Managing Your Most Difficult Customers

Dennis J. Rourke

A Service of

NAHB

BuilderBooks™
National Association of Home Builders
1201 15th Street, NW
Washington, DC 20005-2800
www.builderbooks.com

Managing Your Most Difficult Customers
Dennis J. Rourke

ISBN 0-86718-547-3

Cover design by Armen Kojoyian
Printed in the United States of America
Library of Congress data is available.

Disclaimer
This publication is designed to provide accurate and authoritative information in regard to the subject matter covered. It is sold with the understanding that the publisher is not engaged in rendering legal, accounting, or other professional service. If legal advice or other expert assistance is required, the services of a competent professional person should be sought.
—From a Declaration of Principles jointly adopted by a Committee of the American Bar Association and a Committee of Publishers and Associations.

For further information, please contact:
BuilderBooks™
National Association of Home Builders
1201 15th Street, NW
Washington, DC 20005-2800
(800) 223-2665
Check us out online at: www.builderbooks.com

2/03 SLR/ Data Reproductions Corp., 2000

This book is dedicated to the understanding, patience, and determination of those thousands who work hard every day to deliver proactive customer care; those who meet fair and reasonable expectations while managing others who would otherwise unfairly tarnish the reputation of responsible home builders.

ABOUT THE AUTHOR

Dennis Rourke graduated from the American University in Washington, D.C. with a Bachelor of Science degree in Business Administration, with a double major in real estate and business management. He is a land developer, home builder, and author of *The American Home Builder and the Housing Industry, Construction Management for the Residential Project Manager* and *Financing and Cash Management.*

Mr. Rourke built his first house at the age of twenty-two. During his career, he has held senior management positions with both small- to large-volume home building companies, as well as owning and operating his own medium-volume home building and land development company in the metropolitan Washington D.C. market for almost 30 years. His experience has primarily been centered on residential land development, home building, and the major renovations of existing homes. In addition to developing ground, he has built custom homes, custom speculative homes, and production housing of all types across all price ranges. As a home builder, he has earned the reputation of one who is and has been dedicated to quality construction, pro-active customer care, and the well being of his employees. Mr. Rourke considers management practice to be the most critical requirement for success as a home builder.

PREFACE

This book is intended to provide an overview of customer care for the 21st century home builder. It is an academic book written by a home builder that describes in detail, a process designed to manage those customers that are beyond fair and reasonable in their demands, those who pose the most serious threat to the reputation of the home builder. It is part of a "Builder-to-Builder Series," written to help home builders create a culture, develop policies, and establish a processes that will provide proactive customer care. The book will also provide a training aid that will help staff and trade partners understand how they can support a comprehensive, proactive customer care program.

In well-managed home building companies throughout the country, customer care has become a focus every bit as important as the construction process. Builders have come to recognize the importance of providing proactive customer care; that which goes well beyond the required warranty service following the closing. Customer care is the key to maintaining the customer's goodwill and obtaining referral sales. Satisfied customers are a requirement for outstanding sales performance and sales are the life-blood of home building companies.

This topic has always been a critical part of success in home building, but it has recently become even more critical for the home builder. In the past, litigation and governmental regulation has followed breaches by home builders who have failed to meet their responsibilities. Today, independent survey companies like J D Power and Associates are measuring industry performance and publishing results, and the "information age" presents new opportunities for disgruntled homeowners to voice their discontent. In addition to litigation and poor service ratings, yard signs, homeowner picketing, negative Internet messaging, and bad press, all have the ability to destroy a company that lacks the sensitivity or ability to provide proactive customer care.

To be effective, the complete delivery process must be analyzed and then orchestrated to achieve results. Today, everyone involved in a building organization must accept the responsibility for maintaining healthy customer relationships; it must be a comprehensive effort that goes well beyond senior management and the scope of post-settlement warranty service. Employees must maintain a customer focus and keep in mind that customer care includes *everything that happens between a prospect or customer and the company*. An effective customer care program will tie each employee to the customer with the specific goal of maintaining goodwill and obtaining referral sales. Each employee has an impact on customer satisfaction, they must be held accountable, and they must become proactive by applying routines and attitudes that cause things to happen in planned, desirable ways.

FIGURES

CONTENTS

PART I THE CULTURE

The first requirement in initiating a proactive customer care program is to establish a culture that permits every employee to participate and encourages every employee to accept the challenges inherent in such a goal. Well-managed companies begin with strong leadership, a written statement of purpose, and policies that support such an ambitious goal. This customer care program not only provides direction and information for employees, it permeates all printed statements about the company and helps others understand the depth of the company's commitment to the customer.

CHAPTER 1

ESTABLISH A CUSTOMER FOCUS AND EMPOWER EMPLOYEES

THE CULTURE

The proper culture for a home building company intent on providing proactive customer care is one that focuses on the customer and his or her satisfaction. This must be obvious to everyone and demonstrated in both the company's written statements and its actions. At the end of the day, the measure of the company's sincerity and its success will be reflected in the results. Results that will establish a favorable reputation that will help defend against claims that are unfair and unreasonable. The success of a proactive customer care program will be reflected in its building standards and processes, correspondence, service record, letters of recommendation, survey summaries, and the character of its employees.

THE IMPORTANCE OF LEADERSHIP

Leadership drives culture. The culture in every company is primarily established by its owners and senior management staff. Unless the owners and senior staff embrace a culture with a customer focus, it cannot grow and develop. Although some employees may recognize the importance of proactive customer care, it cannot be effectively implemented unless employees have been directed and enabled by the owners and senior managers of the business. The most important prerequisite to establish a culture with a customer focus is quality of leadership at the top. The senior staff must embrace the concept and understand the importance of proactive customer care; it is critical to the success of the organization. Effective leadership is the key to ensuring the highest level of customer care. A service culture begins with the example set by management in its treatment of its customers, staff, and associates.

THE STATEMENT OF PURPOSE

The ABC Building Company is a high-end, semi-custom, niche home builder. Its purpose is to provide income for employees, return on investment, and to accumulate modest financial growth. The Company will do this by measuring demand for a variety of residential construction projects and filling that demand for the benefit of its purchasers, owners, and employees. It is a Company with a customer focus and it is committed to quality construction and proactive customer care.

A statement of purpose should clearly define the company and establish direction that can be easily understood. This statement should identify the customer as a primary focus and stress the importance of customer care. This will serve not only to inform employees, but also to inform others such as owners, investors, homebuyers, and vendors. The above statement is such an example and the following is an appropriate continuation of that example, which might be included in a business plan, policy manual, or training manual:

The Company will seek opportunity by evaluating facts, by establishing a well-conceived plan of action, and then executing that plan in such a way that its management skill, concern for employees, commitment to the customer, and regard for existing neighborhoods will be obvious. The Company will:

1. Be ethical in all matters and attempt to resolve disputes based on what is fair, reasonable, and in the best interest of the community
2. Protect the environment and conserve natural resources wherever possible and at all reasonable costs
3. Cooperate with state and local governmental agencies to protect the interests of the public
4. Demonstrate concern for production quality and job-site safety
5. Encourage employee participation and offer opportunities for self-improvement and an improved quality of life
6. Maintain a professional bearing and participate in community affairs and the affairs of our industry
7. Make every reasonable attempt to provide exceptional customer service, satisfy the reasonable demands of its purchasers and homeowners, and protect their interests wherever possible
8. Make every reasonable effort to pay bills promptly and discount wherever possible
9. Attempt to seek innovative solutions to design, engineering, and management problems except where increased risks seem to outweigh the potential benefits of such innovation
10. Hire and train employees who are professional, respectful, and courteous to one another at all times

The goal of this Company is to build homes that reflect fine architectural and finish detail, to maintain a quality production process, and to provide proactive customer care. This goal will be accomplished in the following ways:

1. By inviting accountability
2. By incorporating uncompromising quality in everything that is undertaken

3. By creating value through a balance of location, product, price and customer support
4. By setting expectations for our customers and then exceed those expectations
5. By instilling and reinforcing confidence in the Company with our customers and partners
6. By maintaining a culture that promotes positive relationships with our customers and respect for our employees
7. By promoting a balanced life for our employees

Statements such as these are powerful. They not only convey a strong commitment on the part of the company, they provide a way to convey those commitments to employees and others. Such statements set the stage for extraordinary performance by enabling every employee to participate in the process. They also clearly establish the intent of the owners and senior managers for the benefit of others, who may have an interest down the road. These statements demonstrate the intent of the company for the benefit of an investigator, arbitrator, or judge who may become involved in dispute resolution at some time in the future. Such statements, when accompanied by a history of measured performance, are invaluable expressions of the character of a company.

POLICY

Policy is largely the result of operating strategies that have been established by the company. Policy, procedures, and processes are all methods or tactics that are used to implement the business strategies of a company. By creating policies that reinforce the statements of purpose and other business strategies of a company, management develops the plan upon which to execute those strategies; it is the daily procedures, processes, and activities that make the business strategies a reality. Some points of interest included in the service policies of companies with proactive customer care are listed:

◆ Be professional in all matters—This may include uniforms for service technicians, but more importantly, it refers to the attitudes of employees when dealing with very difficult customers. Conversation must center on facts, with as little emotion as possible, and every reasonable effort must be made to satisfy the demands of the customer or inform them of the company's position—regardless of how they are presented by the customer.

◆ Remove post-settlement activities from construction managers and establish a post-settlement service department. Warranty service is time consuming and requires a very high degree of communication with the customer. Construction managers lack the time and patience to satisfy reasonable requirements to maintain favorable customer relationships. Their days are more than filled with the responsibilities related to cycle-time, construction quality, oversight, and shepherding purchasers through the construction process. The responsibility for post-settlement service simply should not be theirs.

◆ Create a clean break between construction and post-settlement service responsibilities. Most home builders require the on-site construction manager to maintain responsibility until the punch list, which is typically prepared at orientation, has been completed; once orientation list is complete, responsibility for customer service becomes the responsibility of the service department. In some cases, home builders have successfully removed responsibility from the on-site construction manager following a "manager's walk" prior to the orientation; in those cases, the service department accepts responsibility for the orientation and the resulting list. In any event, punch lists must be completed quickly, prior to occupancy.

◆ Use construction managers to help evaluate structural issues—Structural issues that develop both during construction, and sometimes after a home has been delivered, should be evaluated first by a knowledgeable construction manager. In most cases, service technicians lack the knowledge and experience necessary to evaluate such conditions. Construction managers should be used first and then, a structural engineer may be required.

◆ Avoid conflict with both purchasers and homeowners through a higher level of communication. Requiring sales managers and service coordinators to communicate with customers, for the express purpose of providing information and checking levels of satisfaction, ensures satisfactory performance. *In the case of the tough customer, such follow-up phone calls should be documented.*

◆ Document and maintain permanent files on all service activities. Documents should include a well-directed letter-writing campaign that covers the construction and service processes, service policy, and letters that indicate a fair and reasonable position in response to unreasonable requests; standard forms resulting from construction meetings, orientation lists, service requests, inspection reports, and other written responses; and follow-up phone calls, survey responses, and third-party inspection reports that have been initiated by either the purchaser/owner or the Company.

◆ Maintain a tracking system to ensure timely and accurate responses to all service requests. Without a tracking system with standardize reporting, a volume building company cannot control the post-settlement process and ensure the timely and complete delivery of service. Such systems confirm a company's commitment to service.

◆ Follow-up all trade contractor or supplier service appointments—The company must be prepared to confirm the timely response and satisfactory completion of open service items. This means that in cases where trade contractors are responsible, the company must confirm completion and customer satisfaction.

◆ Document the refusal of a vendor to undertake a non-covered service request. Require trade contractors and suppliers who evaluate conditions and refuse service requests that are not covered by the warranty to document such positions in writing for the file. This can be a very simple form letter that establishes a third-party position.

◆ Use surveys and follow-up phone calling. These are tools that are used to gain additional information about the product and processes as well as the performance of individual employees responsible for sales, construction, and customer care.

◆ Develop support networks with homeowners within in communities where the company is active. Sponsor and participate in a block party or community meeting early to help maintain goodwill and provide ongoing communication. The only thing most of these homeowners have in common to talk about is the builder, and a difficult customer can create an ugly situation quickly given the opportunity. Use community leaders as examples when dealing with the tough customer

◆ Be proactive and maintain a favorable relationship with local building officials. Have the senior production manager meet with the head of the local building department and discuss policies related to construction and customer care. Open a direct line of communication; they will undoubtedly receive complaints from your tough customers, and it is much better to have established the process up front.

◆ Move the tough customers up the chain. Senior employees are better equipped to manage the tough customers. They should have the experience and skills that others may lack.

◆ Third-party inspectors representing a contract purchaser should be welcome. Most home builders feel that third-party inspectors are an unnecessary financial burden for homebuyers and should be avoided, but, in fact, they are a required part of the process in those cases in which the purchaser feels insecure. A provision in the contract that requires the builder's knowledge and approval before such inspections ensures the builder's right to object to any specific inspection. In the event that a particular inspector is overly aggressive or unfair, the builder can help repair the customer relationship.

WHO PROVIDES CUSTOMER CARE?

Every employee is expected to participate in the delivery of customer care, and performance reviews should include evaluations of each employee's contribution. In well-managed companies, employees are empowered by the written documents that create the direction and policies of the company. Statements of purpose, policy statements, descriptions of the various operating processes used by home builders, and job descriptions all provide the employee with the information that he or she requires to participate.

When employees are empowered and encouraged to provide customer care, management must recognize each will contribute in accordance with his or her understanding, ability, and personal judgment. Training and individual growth and development become critical. To inform employees and help them embrace the culture, they must be trained. This is best accomplished through individual orientations, outside seminars, internal training seminars, and departmental reinforcement in regular staff meetings.

The most difficult customers must ultimately become the responsibility of those managers who have the greatest skill. Moving the most difficult customers up the chain ensures a higher level of performance when dealing with these individuals. With this special group of customers, interpersonal skills, the ability to communicate both orally and in writing, and the proper respect for documentation become critical. If the process is well established, dealing with difficult customers will be easier despite potential risks that they represent to a home builder.

WHO SHOULD BE RESPONSIBLE FOR CUSTOMER CARE?

While every employee should accept the responsibility to provide customer care, one senior level employee should be responsible for the implementation of an effective customer care program. In companies building more than one hundred units per year, this function should be the responsibility of the President or a Vice President at the local level; perhaps, a Vice President of Operations; in larger companies, it is often the responsibility of a Regional VP in national companies. This senior employee must not be associated with the sales, construction, or post-settlement service departments. Most serious complaints focus on the performance of these departments, and an impartial senior manager eliminates the potential for a defensive response and helps the customer feel more comfortable.

A very senior person should demonstrate that a decision at this level is firm and final; this is particularly important with those customers who are unfair and unreasonable. Any attempt by a customer to go around this employee must be refused by owners or corporate executives; **any such demands must be referred back to the senior individual with the responsibility.** If customers are successful going around the senior staff member who is responsible, it creates an unfair solution for those unreasonable owners or purchasers. Owners should monitor results, audit processes, and maintain confidence in the employee who is assigned to the task. For those purposes, owners should review lot files (particularly for the toughest customers) and consider the routine documentation of customer care; it is the best indicator of the success of a proactive program.

In large national or regional corporations, customer care should also be the responsibility of a senior officer at the corporate level and a Vice President at the regional level. The most difficult customers will find ways to carry their complaints to the regional or corporate level, and there must be a provision, which is consistent with an overall customer care program, to deal with them. Unless the company provides reasonable protections for its local staff, complaints that circumvent those who are responsible at the local level will become overwhelming. By providing for a response system in advance, the company can serve the customer, protect its employees, and insure against a potential failure in its customer service delivery program. It is critical to the success of the customer care program that each employee, from the most senior to the least senior, provides care with the same commitment, policies, and process. This will produce consistency and promote internal understanding. Each employee must accept the fact that not all customers will be satisfied regardless of the extraordinary effort on the part of the company.

In most cases, post-settlement warranty service should be directed by the most senior construction manager; in the case of a large company, this individual may be a Vice President of Production with responsibility for construction, purchasing, and warranty service. Experience indicates that by combining these departments under a single head, interdepartmental friction can be avoided. On the other hand, such a consolidation will only work if the warranty service policies and processes are clearly defined and the company audits operations and measures results through surveys.

EMPOWER EMPLOYEES

Companies must empower employees and others who welcome responsibility and accept accountability; they must encourage good communication and cooperation among all staff members and department heads; employees must also maintain a high level of awareness of quality and service issues, learn from mistakes, and celebrate success. Employees are empowered in three ways: 1) through policy, 2) through financial planning, and 3) through a well-organized training program.

THE IMPORTANCE OF POLICY

Policy is important because it sets standards and enables employees to act as advocated for customers. Policies should be organized in a simple format that is easily understood and then published in a manual and posted in a public file on the company server. Access to such documents must be easy for employees, and modifications should be made on a regular basis. Most companies will elect to formally modify policy once a year, and more and more companies are offering employees the opportunity to provide input, participate in the debate, and affect changes where it is in the best interest of the company.

Be professional at all times. Never become emotional, always be respectful, respond firmly if it is appropriate, and never take abuse. Never make any comment or suggestion that would reflect poorly if played back in court or in an arbitration. In the event that a customer has become abusive, it is probably a good idea to document it with a letter unless some forgiveness is in order.

The example on the following page is a very simple but effective format for policy presentation that might be used by a home building company.

RECOGNIZING THE COST

The cost of proactive customer care must be recognized by management and provided for in budgets. A well-defined delivery system, such as the one outlined in this book, creates operating efficiencies, reduces overall cost of construction and callbacks, promotes a higher level of participation on the part of trade contractors, and slightly reduces the overall general and administrative costs. These savings, however, are hard to measure and will not be reflected in the post-settlement service budget. A foundation of this process is the commitment to over-service; it is a commitment to provide a level of service that is indisputable and easily recognized by outside third parties.

Over-service can increase indirect and general administrative costs due to performance bonuses—for construction managers based on quality, condition at delivery, and customer satisfaction; for service technicians based on performance efficiency and customer satisfaction; and for middle managers based on efficiency and customer satisfaction. Bonuses are the best vehicle to maintain a high degree of focus on customer care. Such bonuses improve employee total compensation, and they help justify the need for accountability. They should reward exceptional performance.

A TRAINING PROGRAM

To improve the level of individual performance in the area of customer care, the company must institute a training program. Nothing will help develop a culture of proactive customer care quicker than a well-directed training program. It is not necessary for a training program to consume a great deal of time, but it must be well conceived and supported by senior staff. Training can be accomplished in the following ways:

STANDARD POLICIES AND PROCEDURES THE ABC BUILDING COMPANY, INC.	Date of Implementation: _____ Departmental V.P.: _____ President: _____

ENTRY POLICY AND WORK STATUS REPORT

Purpose: The purpose of this policy is to memorialize entry and key policies, and to provide a means for improved communications with homeowners regarding service work performed in their homes.

Entry Policy

Under no circumstances shall a single technician enter a house to perform work if an unattended minor child is present. If this situation arises then the technician must get a second employee to assist him/her during the performance of such work.

If any pre-existing damage to the residence is evident prior to the start of work and not covered by the warranty, the technician is to photograph the damage, leave the unit and notify the Customer Care Coordinator immediately. Work will not resume until the homeowner has been contacted and advised of the pre-existing condition.

In the event that damage is caused to a unit, or its contents, by a Company service employee, the Customer Care Coordinator is to be notified immediately. A photograph of the damage is to be taken and sent to the office with a copy of the damage report.

Key Policy

Although the Company policy is to avoid accepting keys from homeowners in order to secure access for service work, there are times when this is necessary. On these occasions the **Consent to Access and Release** form **MUST BE SIGNED PRIOR TO ENTERING** the house and the Customer Care Coordinator must notify the homeowner prior to the scheduled work date.

Work Status Report

When it becomes necessary to work in a home when the homeowner is not there, a "Work Status Report" shall be filled out and left on the kitchen counter. This will help avoid confusion and improve the lines of communication. A copy of the report must then be stapled to the Service Work Order for submission to the main office for permanent filing.

In the case of exterior work, the homeowner shall be notified by use of a door hanger. In such event, the top (white) copy of the door hanger must be submitted to the office with the Service Work Order for inclusion in the permanent lot file.

FIGURE 1.1. Standard policies and procedures for the ABC Building Company, Inc.

◆ Orientation at employment—A senior staff member must meet with each new employee within the first few days and cover the basic policies, procedures, and processes that insure a high level of customer care. New employees must understand the importance of customer care, that they will be held accountable for it, and that their success with the company will depend on it.

◆ Internal training seminars—In larger companies, such seminars can easily be managed by breaking the company into two or more groups and staggering the sessions. These seminars should be conducted once or twice each year depending on the size of the company and the volume of new hires.

◆ Departmental meetings—Customer care should be a separate agenda item for departmental meetings at least once each quarter. The focus should be on current performance levels and areas requiring improvement. Teaming is a big part of an effective customer care program and each employee must be able to rely on consistency in the application of policies, procedures, and processes. This is a point that must be reinforced in departmental meetings; the policies, procedures, and processes must be discussed; and each employee must be extended the opportunity to offer suggestions for improvement.

Try never to say "no." Offer a reasonable compromise, offer an alternative, or provide assistance in some way. This is particularly important when a customer demands service that is not covered by the warranty. In many cases, it will be as simple as recommending a tradesman or contractor that might be willing to work directly for the homeowner. Often, these customers simply have no way to get it done.

◆ Senior staff meetings—Such meetings offer a perfect opportunity to reinforce the customer care program. Senior staff must focus on the current level of performance, make adjustments wherever necessary, and acknowledge outstanding performers. The senior employee responsible for customer care should make a formal presentation each quarter, present the results of surveys and follow-up phone calling, and initiate a discussion related to improvement.

◆ Annual, semi-annual, or quarterly company meetings— Customer care should be a separate agenda item for these meetings and include a report on the results of satisfaction surveys for the prior quarter and the last 12 months.

Be consistent. Never do something for one homeowner that you would not be willing to do for another. Be prepared to defend your solutions. Would an unbiased third party say this solution was fair and reasonable? Would other homeowners say that you were showing favoritism or buying off a difficult customer? Sometimes it is easier to simply say that you cannot do something for one that you would not be willing to do for everyone.

◆ Partnership meetings for trade contractors and suppliers—Partnership meetings provide an exceptional opportunity to help others understand the depth of the company's commitment and to solicit each vendor's support.

A varied and simple training program such as this can be very effective. Often it is simply enough to focus on the goals, measure and evaluate the results, and encourage others to participate.

TEACHING PATIENCE

Effective communication with purchasers and homeowners requires patience and understanding. Any contact with customers must not be rushed; except in very unusual cases, the employee must listen carefully, establish rapport, and find out how he or she can help. Because such communication can be time consuming, customer contact with on-site construction managers should be limited. This can only occur if other employees help protect the construction manager from unnecessary distractions. In medium to large building companies, the sales manager should always be the contact person; it is his or her job to shepherd the customer through the sales, construction, and settlement process. Following settlement, the customer becomes the responsibility of the customer care coordinator.

It will be very difficult to teach project managers and superintendents to exhibit the degree of patience necessary for close customer contact. They are production people, and it is their impatience and "get it done" personalities that help them meet cycle-time requirements. They must, however, exhibit a high degree of patience during those few occasions when they are working with the customer.

ACCOUNTABILITY

Each employee must accept responsibility for proactive customer care, and they must understand that they will be held accountable for the quality of their effort. It will be measured and discussed during performance reviews, additional compensation will depend on it, and homeowners will be asked to evaluate it on a very personal level. On-site sales managers, construction managers, and service technicians will be the subject of specific questions in satisfaction surveys; homeowners will be asked to evaluate them in terms of their willingness to provide customer care.

Anytime you ask an employee to be accountable for customer care, you must recognize that your toughest customers may not be satisfied regardless of the effort, and even worse, some will make it their duty to discredit hard-working, well-intentioned employees. At these times, the general staff and management must consider the facts with the knowledge that some customers require a much higher level of management; they must resist the tendency to assume that the employee has breached any responsibility either to the company or to the customer. The real questions are: Was the employee acting within the process? Did the employee follow policy? Did the employee remain professional? What is the history of this customer? Although frustration can cause a well-meaning employee to lose control with a tough customer, in well-managed companies with proactive customer care programs, it will usually be the customer who is unfair and unreasonable.

CHAPTER 2

UNDERSTAND THE MISSION AND THE POTENTIAL FOR SUCCESS

The customer care process that is outlined in this book springs from three basic beliefs that are as follows:

1. **Customer care is circular in nature and not linear.** There is no end to the service that home builders will provide to customers over the life of the relationship. Although post-settlement service responsibilities usually terminate at the end of the first full year following closing (except as it may relate to plumbing, mechanical, electrical, or structural conditions), providing advice, information, or general assistance to customers continues. The Pulte Corporation refers to this as their Customer for Life Program.

2. **In well-managed companies with responsible service policies and reasonable performance, ten percent of the home buying population will rate the builder as "poor."** This fact was supported by information provided by J.D. Power and Associates in a seminar at the National Association of Home Builders (NAHB) International Builder's Conference four years ago. This population is the central problem of responsible home builders today. The builder's most difficult customers can be found in this group. With the right process, the majority of this group will become quiet, which leaves approximately two percent that will continue to be vocal and threatening. It is this two percent that can destroy a responsible home builder, and at a minimum, damage the reputation and cause great hardship for staff.

3. **Home builders and their staff must place more emphasis on the remaining ninety percent.** Too often, the majority of the resources are committed to the dissatisfied small group, without proper regard for those who, with a little effort will move the company to a new level in customer satisfaction. Unless the company maintains a deliberate process for the delivery of proactive customer care, it will not achieve its full potential with regard to goodwill and referral sales.

An unreasonable focus on the most difficult customers, who will never rate the builder better than poor, creates an unfair position for other homeowners and staff. Other homeowners eventually come to realize that this group is unreasonable, and they resent any special consideration given to them; and conversely, they admire a company with policies that protect their interests. Any attempt by senior management to embrace the unreasonable demands and hostile behavior of this group can demoralize staff and cause them to resent such actions. This can be particularly harmful to those who are expected to manage this group on a day-to-day basis.

THE CONSUMER CROSS-SECTION

J.D. Power and Associates, a leading global marketing information company, has collected significant customer service data for the homebuilding industry. For a typical well-managed home building company, 10% of customers will rate the home builder as poor, regardless of any efforts; 80% will rate the home builder as below average, average, or above average; and 10% will rate a home builder as great, for reasons the builder may never understand.

Most builders find themselves working to satisfy the middle 80 percent, hoping that with little effort, below-average ratings will increase to average, and average ratings will increase to above average. This is the focus of a well-managed customer service department. Obviously, the top 10 percent should never be taken for granted. But, what is to be done with the 10 percent of those who would rate a home builder as poor? Through manipulation, bad press, and litigation, this group can cripple the success of a home builder.

By concentrating on the customer service delivery system, you can reduce this problematic 10 percent of customers. Create a culture, policy, procedure, and process that effectively manages the entire customer service spectrum. Treat customers with respect and over-service, and let the process take care of the lowest 10 %. Have your customer service managers focus on the 80%, who, with a little effort, will move your rating from below average to average, from average to above average, or from average to great. This is the real focus of customer care.

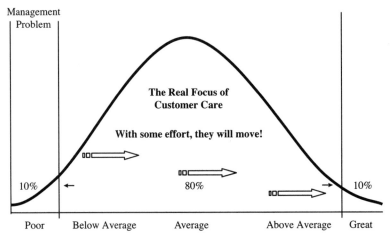

FIGURE 2.1. Well-managed builder performance rating for typical new homeowner population. Builders should concentrate on the 80% who, with a little effort, will move your rating from below average to average, from average to above average, and from above average to great. This is the real focus of customer care.

THE TOP TEN PERCENT

This group of customers would say the company is great. These homeowners may have purchased late in the construction cycle, they are typically positive people, or they may have expected less. It is hard to say. This group does not receive a higher level of service than that other experience. They are people who achieve success through positive action and positive thinking. They are a gift, and we must never betray their confidence.

THOSE IN THE MIDDLE

This group would say the company is below average, average, or above average. This group is composed of people like us; they are fair reasonable people who require customer care in varying degrees. They are people who are more than willing to make some reasonable accommodations as long as they feel you are acting in good faith and sincerely want to do the right thing. A little well-directed attention will go a long way with this group. We must recognize their needs and work hard to accommodate them. **This is where success in customer satisfaction is won or lost.**

Understand that response time is critical. Acknowledge requests for warranty service immediately. It is also helpful to accept formal requests for service on a standard form by mail, fax, email, or directly through an Internet site. Make it easy, and your customers will be less disappointed.

THE BOTTOM TEN PERCENT

This group would say the company is poor. This is the group that creates internal friction. They produce a high degree of stress and insecurity in dedicated employees; they demand out of schedule service; they cause management to doubt the effectiveness of their employees; they require a much higher degree of management; and they require considerable research, letter writing, and legal coordination. Even in companies that offer proactive customer care, this group can consume as much as fifty percent of your resources, if you let them. Without a process that captures these customers early and manages them throughout the process, considerable time and effort will be wasted, and a large portion of your staff may become demoralized or stressed out.

THE J D POWER EXPERIENCE

J.D. Power and Associates recently completed a study that evaluated 282 home builders across 10 major markets, with responses from more than 45,000 buyers in newly constructed homes. They concluded there are nine factors that drive overall customer satisfaction with home builders.

These top four items comprise 70% of all responses:

1. Customer service   23 %
2. Home readiness   18 %

3.	Sales staff	16 %
4.	Quality of workmanship/materials	<u>14 %</u>
	Subtotal	71 %

The remaining five factors were the following:

5.	Price/value	10 %
6.	Physical design elements	7 %
7.	Design center	5 %
8.	Recreational facilities	4 %
9.	Location	<u>3 %</u>
	Total	100 %

According to the company "The study indicates that while some of these remaining factors are very important when homebuyers are selecting a builder, they become less important once the homebuyer occupies the home." After an evaluation of the results, Paula Sonkin, the Senior Director of Real Estate Industries Practice, stated "Every additional contact required between homeowner and builder to solve a problem tends to result in lower satisfaction with the builder. It's definitely in the best interest of the builder to get it right the first time."

Builders can expect the work of J.D. Power to continue, and the results of their surveys will impact sales for volume home builders. If your company scores low in the rankings in your market, expect a negative sales reaction, and conversely, if it scores high, expect greater sales success.

THE REAL POTENTIAL FOR SUCCESS

We can't satisfy everyone. Companies that approach customer service with the expectation they will achieve a 98 percent referral rate are simply not realistic and often abuse their employees in the attempt. Each employee should make every reasonable effort to preserve the customer's goodwill and obtain his or her referral; this is our responsibility, and it is a key measure of ethical behavior. The commitment of the company, its policies, processes, and the performance of its employees should also be measured to determine the success of a customer service program. It is not just a question of what our customers think; it is more a matter of what we know as professionals about our delivery system and our ability to manage the tough ones. Those who rank high in customer care already know this. This is the combination that creates an outstanding reputation. It is not easy for a competitor to duplicate your reputation in the short-term; an outstanding reputation is built slowly.

The real problem is recognizing the truly difficult customers from others with reasonable complaints. The foundation for this process is built on understanding, quality construction, documentation effort, control conditions, and a higher level of customer care for all. Those who learn to manage this group will gain the respect of other homeowners within the same community. This group may fool their neighbors for a while, but eventually their neighbors come to understand what the builder already knows; these are unfair and unreasonable people. In fact, this group is merely a management problem and should be approached with caution, but without fear.

Purchasing a new home can be a very unsettling experience filled with insecurity, uncertainty, misconceptions, and, sometimes, unreasonable expectations. For many, it is a stressful experience under the best of conditions. Negotiating and contracting is not a great experience for most, and the construction process is probably worse. Disappointment and compromise is not unusual whether the customer is purchasing a starter home, a second or third move-up home, or a custom home. It can be a very difficult experience for those who buy new homes in today's markets. Skilled labor continues to shrink, and home builders continue to struggle with basic quality and fit and finish standards; in some cases, builders are not as well organized as they should be, and in still other cases, communication is poor. So

Document all extra effort that demonstrates a willingness to go beyond what is reasonable:

- *Note any mover damage that was repaired as a courtesy*
- *Create a no-charge change order in cases in which a concession is made as a result of a contract error*
- *Create a service order if you decide to spruce up planting beds that have weathered before occupancy*
- *Use door hangers (with a copy to the file) to let homeowners know that you have done something special*

what does this mean to our buyers? There is a very high potential for trouble.

According to the National Mental Health Association, one in ten of us have some form of mental illness. In the course of a year, more than 40 million adult Americans are affected by one or more mental disorders, and 6.5 million suffer from severe mental illnesses. In fact, according to NMHA, nearly two-thirds of all people with diagnosable mental disorders do not seek treatment. These are extraordinary statistics. Unless we approach this group with understanding and compassion, we do a great disservice to a large number of people. In a company committed to proactive customer care, employees must understand with whom they are dealing and what is truly possible.

There are five major categories of mental illness, and anyone working with the public should be aware of them:

1. Anxiety disorders: phobias, panic disorders, and obsessive-compulsive disorders
2. Mood disorders: depression and bipolar disorders
3. Schizophrenia
4. Dementias
5. Eating disorders

Home builders and their staff must be prepared to help everyone. They must be compassionate, understanding, and supportive; they must be direct, consistent, and respectful; and they must document their effort and the behavior of their customers carefully.

Home builders also seem to be a target for those who have a high propensity for litigation. Most of these purchasers will only "jump ugly" if they are under stress. The smart ones know how to create considerable inconvenience and expense for the homebuilder. The most deadly combination for a homebuilder is a two percenter (2%'er) who is an attorney; these purchasers will undoubtedly increase legal fees and create considerable embarrassment, but if the builder has effectively implemented a proactive customer care program, even they can be defeated. Extreme caution must be exercised with these purchasers because they will try to mobilize the neighborhood against you to create a class action suit; in most cases, new homeowners will give them a platform, and many will assume they are suitable leaders.

Home builders who are struggling with a purchaser who is aggressive, as well as unfair and unreasonable, are probably better off working through the purchaser's attorney. In fact, after a threat of litigation, the customer should have his or her attorney call the builder. If the company can document its ongoing efforts to over-service the customer, to be fair and reasonable in the resolution of complaints or disputes, produce documents that validate its success with other customers, and demonstrate its willingness to do the right thing, the prospects of litigation often disappear. Most attorneys, like most of our purchasers are fair reasonable people, and they recognize unfair and unreasonable demands. Such demands do not play well in court if the history is well documented. The same experience can be said for arbitration; if the builder is armed with documentation, and the facts show the company has been fair and reasonable, arbitration may be the best way to close responsibilities with a tough customer.

MANAGING THOSE WHO RATE US POORLY

It is the responsible of management to deal with the most difficult two percent. If the company is organized to overcome the attacks by those who are unfair and unreasonable, the staff will have more time to focus on the eighty percent, who are the real target of customer care.

These difficult customers are usually identified early, but all too often, the employee will attempt to manage them without the necessary skills; this can sometimes lead to an even larger problem. The company must establish a policy that moves the responsibility of managing these customers up the chain; those with more senior positions have greater skills to deal with the problems. Their responses protect the company, their communication skills may be better, their authority to make decisions is greater, and they are better able to take a firm position.

However, in most companies, the front-line employees feel they have somehow failed if they do not manage these customers. In a proactive company, senior management makes this clear to their customer service managers. Believe me, all of these customers will find their way to the top; you'll see faster resolution if you control the communications early in the process. Sales managers, service managers, construction managers, and administrators must maintain composure and their professionalism as they work with customers. They must not be allowed to become demoralized or discouraged by their inability to satisfy these tough customers; the management of these customers is the responsibility of those at the top.

What then becomes of these customers? It is simple; customer care is circular for everyone else, but it is linear for these people. That is, in well-managed and responsible companies, customer service never ends; it is circular and, while the company may not come with tools, it will always be available to help its customers no matter how long they have lived in their homes. For unfair and unreasonable customers, service will expire after 14 to 18 months following settlement, with the exception of electrical, plumbing, mechanical, and structural items that go beyond the first year. The senior manager should ensure the following: 1) the records are in order; 2) the customer has received the very highest level of warranty service; 3) the company has made every reasonable effort to resolve disputes fairly; and 4) the behavior of the customer has been well documented. At that point, senior management should send a letter informing the customer that the company will no longer respond to unreasonable demands. Such letters must be very carefully crafted and may become a central focus in litigation or arbitration. The following is an example of such a letter:

The ABC Building Company, Inc.
1234 Anyplace Drive
Rockville, MD 20854

December 6, 2002

John Q. and Mary A. Customer
4567 Baywood Court
Fairfax, VA 22180

Dear Mr. and Mrs. Customer:

   After repeated efforts to satisfy your unreasonable demands, we are frustrated and disappointed. In the sixteen months since you closed on your new home, we have attended to more than three hundred and fifty-one (351) items which you have submitted on six separate service lists beginning with the list dated June 2000. As I have indicated both in conversation and in writing, this company takes great pride in its proactive customer care program, and we will do anything within reason to preserve the goodwill of our customers. We clearly understand that our future depends on our efforts to satisfy our customers, but in your case, it is clear to us that this cannot be accomplished. In spite of our efforts, you continue to make unreasonable demands, discredit us in the community, and threaten us with litigation and bad press.

   As a result of this impasse, I have made the decision that we will no longer respond to your unreasonable requests, except as it relates to structural, plumbing, or mechanical warranties. Electrical, plumbing and mechanical warranties will expire in June of next year and your structural coverage will continue until May of 2010. I sincerely regret having made this decision, but it is clear to us that you will never consider us anything better than poor, and there is little incentive for us to continue providing a level of customer service that is neither appreciated nor warranted. I want you both to understand that this Company will continue to hope for your happiness and support you in this community, but we cannot continue responding to your unreasonable demands.

Respectfully,

William C. Smith
President

c.c. Robert F. Jones, Esq.

FIGURE 2.2. Unreasonable demands letter.

For obvious reasons, this is a letter that can only be written by the most senior manager responsible for customer care (ideally, the President or a Vice President of the company), and it must be written with the full knowledge and consent of the owners and an attorney. In most cases, the homeowner will respond by phone to discuss the matter. The senior manager must be prepared for this; he or she must have considered this possibility and prepared himself or herself to be professional, supportive, but firm in response.

THE DANGER OF ANTICIPATING

Unless we are committed to providing professional and calculated service for *every* homebuyer, we run the risk of creating a failure in the process. Do not anticipate the difficult customers; treat everyone with respect and let the process work. Recognize the most difficult customers, but do not treat them differently.

To assume that a customer is unfair or unreasonable before a history has been established is a fool's mistake, and it will undoubtedly expose the company to a level of liability that is unacceptable.

Every employee must recognize the extraordinary liability that comes with a dissatisfied customer—with or without legitimate complaints. Jury awards and the cost of litigation are significant.

To manage customers, employees must remain professional and let the system work.

Part II The Requirements

A proactive customer care process must include a well-coordinated sales effort, a quality building program, an effective orientation, extraordinary post-settlement service, and a unique commitment on the part of staff. These are the unique elements that create positive references in the minds of both homebuyers and homeowners. These elements help customers develop the confidence they need to overcome the confusion and frustration that is part of the production and post-settlement service processes. It is also the basis for a home building company to demonstrate the extent of its commitment to its buyers. Builders must design quality in both the homes they build and the services they provide. Customer satisfaction is achieved when both product and services respond to the needs of customers—needs that include product quality and proactive customer care.

CHAPTER 3

A QUALITY BUILDING PROGRAM AND EXTRAORDINARY POST-SETTLEMENT SERVICE

WELL-COORDINATED SALES EFFORT

All too often, the collateral material and standard option pricing used to market new homes is inadequate and does not reflect the current plans and building standards. Standard option descriptions are nonexistent or they are loosely constructed and create enormous potential for misunderstanding. Coordinating the collateral marketing material, option descriptions, and option pricing with the actual construction and purchasing process is essential to reduce confusion and the potential for significant disputes with homebuyers. In cases in which plans, specifications, and standard options are not well thought out, reprints, re-pricing, and display adjustments become necessary and create confusion in the minds of buyers. To overcome the contingent liability created by poorly coordinated marketing materials, both the sales and production departments must participate in new product development, and procedures must insure that future changes are not made unilaterally. Product development and marketing programs must be coordinated with a great deal of thought up front. Where this does not occur, marketing soft costs increase, and unnecessary confusion and frustration are created for purchasers. Home builders must take the time to understand their markets and develop their products carefully to eliminate these unnecessary costs and the potential for conflict. These typical mistakes, made by home builders, have significant consequences on the attitudes of purchasers:

STANDARD FEATURE SHEETS

◆ Statements that are technically inaccurate, particularly as they relate to material applications

◆ Options that are listed as a standard features; this often results from a change after the product has been introduced to the market

◆ Listing of a standard feature that could not be successfully executed in actual construction; this often results from a construction failure to execute the original concept during model construction

◆ Description of a feature that has been eliminated in actual construction; this often results from field changes made to improve the process

◆ General site plan descriptions or statements that are not consistent for every lot; broad statements that do not apply to every site

FLOOR PLANS AND ELEVATIONS

◆ Error in room dimensions

◆ Inaccuracy between the plan and the illustration; this is often a coordination error resulting from the illustrators lack of construction experience

◆ Presentation of an elevation that is not available

◆ Floor plan errors that do not reflect actual construction; often the result of field changes or a failure to execute the plan properly in model construction

◆ Illustration of an exterior material that is not available

PRODUCT DISPLAYS

◆ Displaying products that have been discontinued; this results from a failure to keep marketing material current

◆ Displaying upgrade products as standard selections

◆ Failure to make all standard or upgrade selections available to every purchaser

◆ Substantial color variations between the display and the actual material; in most cases, this is normal, but no attempt to provide a disclaimer can cause conflict

OPTION DESCRIPTIONS AND PRICING

◆ Inaccurate descriptions that overstate the option

◆ Descriptions that are vague and leave considerable room for conceptual errors

◆ Descriptions that do not fully describe the execution of the option

◆ Pricing that exceeds what the purchaser perceives as fair or reasonable; this is particularly true of appliance and flooring upgrades

◆ Poorly defined pricing process that creates unusual delays and confusion

CONTRACT RATIFICATION PROCESS

◆ Unnecessary delays in contract presentation

◆ Delays resulting from extended reviews; this can occur when the process requires multiple reviews by various department heads

◆ Counteroffers that are not anticipated by the purchaser

CONTRACT DOCUMENTS

◆ Documents that are poorly coordinated and do not afford the basic and reasonable protections that the builder requires

◆ Documents that do not require arbitration (in states where it is available), approval for third-party inspections, or controlled site inspections by the purchaser

◆ Incomplete contract documents; this creates the need to go back to the purchaser for the execution of additional documents

◆ Contracts that lack clarity in addendum language

◆ Legal errors in document preparation that might create a dispute or void the contract

◆ Statements that are unclear, create contingencies, or provide extraordinary conditions of sale

◆ Errors in pricing

◆ Guaranteed delivery dates

◆ Failure to provide a sample warranty and warranty standards

NON-STANDARD OPTION PROCESS

◆ Inadequate descriptions; can cause confusion and delays in pricing

◆ Loose pricing process that creates extraordinary delays

◆ Reluctance to reject the option request quickly when it is an unreasonable condition or does not meet the criteria for execution

ADVERTISING

◆ Misrepresentation of material facts

◆ Statements that are misleading

◆ Graphics that do not reflect actual conditions of construction or the community

A QUALITY BUILDING PROGRAM

A quality building program not only reduces callbacks and risks related to product liability and on-site safety, it also provides a higher level of confidence for both consumers and staff; it reduces unnecessary costs and delays related to corrections or repairs late in the production process. A quality building program is necessary to satisfy customers and reduce construction costs for both the home builder and vendors. Building a quality product and documenting it fends off those who might otherwise criticize unfairly.

Always respond to customer complaints quickly and in writing. This is particularly true when the customer has involved Government Officials, the Office of Consumer Affairs, the Building Department, or the Home Builders Association. These third parties will all open a file and want to document the resolution. Keep them informed and take the opportunity to teach them the value of your process.

A quality building program consists of eight major requirements: 1) well-qualified staff, 2) uniform contracts, specifications and scopes of work, 3) use of engineers, 4) involvement with customers, 5) frame checks and floor checks, 6) quality assurance program, 7) oversight inspections, and 8) partnership program for trade contractors and suppliers.

WELL-QUALIFIED STAFF

Production staff must be well qualified. Some years ago, superintendents were used to manage residential construction sites. These employees were largely responsible for the oversight of the various trades working on the project. Today, the responsibilities of these on-site construction managers are much more complicated. They must not only provide the oversight for the trades, who are poorly trained in many cases, but they must also play a critical role in planning, purchasing, and sales coordination, as well as providing proactive customer care. These are complicated positions and require a much higher level of management expertise and communication skills.

Key construction managers must be experienced with the ability to anticipate and prevent problems; they must be good problem solvers, and they must be able to maintain good customer relationships. They must be knowledgeable when it comes to Building Codes and Industry Standards; they must understand effective methods of construction management; and they must be able to maintain schedules and the quality of construction. They must have *good interpersonal skills* and be *committed to a higher level of oversight*. The requirements have never been greater than they are today, but neither have the demands on these key employees.

UNIFORM CONTRACTS, SPECIFICATIONS, AND SCOPES OF WORK

Developing uniform labor and material contracts, project specifications, and scopes of work will help everyone understand the terms and conditions of construction. These basic documents provide a clear understanding of the materials to be used and the responsibilities for construction. When combined with the architectural and engineering plans, they become the enabling documents for construction managers and trade contractors. They provide legal protections along with clear statements related to specific areas of the construction process.

Some builders have gone as far as requiring the painting contractor to vacuum out the house prior to prepping for paint and applying a prime coat on the interior. In well-managed building companies, most quality issues after completion are related to fit and finish. Attempts to improve fit and finish should focus on the scopes of work; by inserting key language in scopes for the core finish trades, a significant improvement can be made.

These documents should be used for management purposes only, and should not be confused with the sales plans and feature sheets that are often used as exhibits and attached to the new home contracts of sale used with purchasers. As management tools, they help employees understand both the product and the construction process. While plans and specifications are often given to purchasers of new custom homes, they should never be given to purchasers of production homes. Such materials have been developed with the product at considerable expense to the company and should be protected; they should only be provided to those who have the need and are part of the production process. General specifications should include the following statement:

> These general specifications have been prepared for internal management purposes only. They are not intended to be used as an attachment to a sales contract for the purchase of a new home; sales specifications have been prepared for that purpose.

USING ENGINEERS

On production projects, soils engineers should be used for all footing inspections, and certifications should be placed in the permanent lot file located in the main office. Structural engineers should also be employed during the product development process and to make field inspections where required. Reports resulting from such field inspections should also be placed in the permanent lot file in the main office. In the event that a truss repair becomes necessary, the certified repair detail should also be placed in the permanent file in the main office. Engineering documentation should be an important part of the lot history and the permanent file (either hard copies or scan files of the documents where electronic files are maintained) should reflect it. In the event that an issue arises after completion, the proper documentation will be available for those responding to the issue.

INVOLVING THE CUSTOMER

Communicating with homebuyers during the construction process is a critical part of providing customer care. It is during this period that purchasers have the most questions and experience the most frustration and anxiety. Every home builder should encourage customer involvement during the construction process. Such involvement should, however, be controlled and in accordance with company policy. In addition to site inspections that may be scheduled by the purchaser, each purchaser should meet with the construction manager or his representative on at least three occasions during the construction process: (1) a *pre-construction meeting* should be scheduled with the project manager and the sales agent for the purpose of discussing the process and reviewing the proposed construction including both standard and non-standard option selections; (2) a *pre-drywall walk* should be conducted by the construction manager prior to concealment for the purpose of reviewing the framing and rough-ins prior to drywall; and, (3) a formal, disciplined, and almost scripted *orientation* should be conducted by the construction or service manager upon completion. The purpose of the orientation is to demonstrate the house, provide information and a discussion of post-settlement service procedures, and finally, to walk the house for the purpose of inspecting fit and finishes throughout. Each inspection should include the execution of a single-page document that memorializes the meeting, the substance of the conversation, and any concerns expressed by the purchaser. In each case, a copy of the report, acknowledged by the purchaser, should be placed in the permanent lot file in order to confirm discussions and document the resolution of issues or questions.

FRAME CHECKS AND FLOOR CHECKS

To ensure a higher level of quality, on-site field construction managers should be required to conduct frame and floor checks. All framing should be checked carefully prior to concealment and all floor sheathing should be checked carefully prior to the application of floor finishes. Using a high-visibility paint and a keel (a heavy marking crayon), framing and floor sheathing should be marked in areas where adjustments are required. Requiring formal frame and floor checks will help reduce minor defects, such as bowed walls and floor squeaks that could become costly repairs after completion.

QUALITY ASSURANCE PROGRAM

An effective quality assurance program for home builders consists of a detailed checklist covering every reasonable concern related to framing and rough-in stage of construction. A typical list might consist of 80 to 100 items set in trade categories that include framing (including windows, exterior doors, and stairs), party-wall construction (where appropriate), HVAC rough, plumbing rough, electrical rough, air stopping, and insulation. This checklist should be reviewed and signed off by the on-site construction manager with a copy to the permanent lot file in the main office. In the event of deficiencies, they should be noted with corrective action. Although most experienced construction managers resist such lists, they can significantly improve the quality of construction, minimize mistakes, reduce costs, and provide evidence of a higher building standard.

OVERSIGHT INSPECTIONS

Oversight is critical for quality in construction. On-site construction managers must walk their houses every day and area construction supervisors must validate both the process and the standards of quality. The work of tradesmen must be inspected for both quality and to insure safe working conditions; materials must be inspected to insure that they meet reasonable standards of quality; and, structural elements must be inspected for performance. Oversight inspections will improve construction quality, protect against waste, and help maintain a safe workplace, as well as inspire a higher level of confidence in homebuyers.

PARTNERSHIP PROGRAM

A number of builders throughout the country are developing partnership programs with core trade contractors and suppliers. These informal relationships are largely based on "best prices" and pro-active support for the builder, with quick pay, a higher level of communication, and higher volume for the vendor. In many cases, the builder will host a luncheon twice a year and present a very carefully prepared production agenda with an emphasis on production flow, critical requirements for improvement, and well directed customer service.

Unless home builders reinforce the need for professional, responsive service with trade contractors and suppliers, the service that these companies provide will be less than desirable. Production builders are in the best position to demand the highest level of customer care from their trade contractors and suppliers, but every home builder must be aware that they can make a difference if they work with their vendors and help direct the quality of service that is provided. In order to support the company's efforts to provide proactive customer care, trade contractors and suppliers must:

◆ Acknowledge the responsibility to provide professional customer service

◆ Organize a delivery system that will insure that only well qualified, trained, and trustworthy tradesmen enter a home

◆ Maintain a high level of communication with the homeowner and demonstrate the highest level of support for the home builder

◆ Follow-up to insure that any complaint is fairly resolved

◆ Guard against the broken appointment, which can only frustrate the homeowner and destroy the goodwill that the builder has worked hard to achieve

In most cases, major suppliers, and plumbing and HVAC contractors maintain service departments with some form of delivery system, but not all core trade contractors understand their responsibilities for customer service. In those cases where service is inadequate or ineffective, the builder must get involved in order to insure the success of his own program.

Every employee involved in the production process must recognize his or her responsibility to maintain quality standards through vigilance. In addition to on- and off-site construction personnel and the on-site sales personnel, all others who play a part in the home building or post-settlement service process must accept the responsibility to support the on-site project manager or superintendent to ensure success. This also means that the on-site project manager or superintendent must be receptive to support from others. In most cases, construction managers must know what an acceptable standard is for the various trades and then inspect the work of every trade to verify conformance. Quality is largely the result of knowledgeable and effective oversight, based on a commitment to see "every single house, every single day." While this may not be practical every day, effective construction managers understand the importance of evaluating the work of each trade as work progresses.

A quality-building program will help the home builder do it right the first time and avoid costly disputes and unnecessary adjustments to finished work after completion. Product quality is often an indicator of a company's ability to compete and the effectiveness of its management practice. A formal process with well-documented effort not only improves quality and reduces costs, but it also reduces the risks of disputes and litigation in an area of operations, in which defending against unreasonable complaints can be very difficult.

PROCESS ENGINEERING

In addition to establishing a quality building program, proactive home builders must also understand the value of process engineering. It can help improve the construction and other processes with some very important benefits for homebuyers. Improvements in the overall home building process benefit the buyer as well as the company. Improving the processes that are part of the overall home building business reduces friction, improves the delivery of customer care, reduces cycle-time, reduces costs, and creates efficiencies that respond to the needs of the company, its homebuyers, its investors, and its strategic partners. Extraordinary benefits can be achieved from a program of ongoing evaluation and improvement.

Process engineering is the science of organizing an activity or series of activities in such a way that goals may be achieved efficiently in the proper sequence of events; it is the establishment of a systematic series of actions directed to the achievement of a specific goal, and it is the application of resources, including labor, material, and equipment, to primary and secondary processes designed to achieve a particular result. Such planning substantially reduces chronic waste and confusion, and it improves construction quality and cycle-time, both of which improve customer confidence and satisfaction. Some of the key elements of process engineering for home builders include the following:

◆ The customer must remain a central focus

◆ Quality must be part of the culture and it is the direct result of planning, control, and ongoing improvement

◆ The cost of implementation must be weighed carefully

◆ Production must be approached with a sense of urgency

◆ Participants must anticipate potential obstacles that will create delays

◆ Trade contractors and other strategic partners must be encouraged to participate in the engineering of the production, sales, and service processes. They can suggest effective methods of managing schedules by improving the process and reducing the required time-line. By encouraging their participation, builders solicit their cooperation, obtain their commitments to work schedules and processes, and validate time-targets. They can also identify weaknesses in an existing process and become part of the problem solving effort and overall process improvement. This is particularly true of trade contractors assisting in the areas of material specifications, methods of material handling, and fastening systems.

◆ The goals and processes must be enforced by employees, as well as trade contractors, suppliers, and other strategic partners

◆ Equipment must be maintained to minimize down-time

◆ The sequence of events must be subject to constant review to ensure that the labor, material, equipment, and other resources are available when they are needed

◆ Exceptional performance must be rewarded

◆ Key trades such as concrete, masonry, carpentry, and drywall have a considerable impact on the overall production schedule, most delays and lost time occur prior to trim, and in cold climates, it becomes critical to coordinate house construction with site development as winter approaches.

◆ The recommendations of warranty service personnel should be taken very seriously

Although most home builders focus more clearly on a quality building program, the secondary processes of home building must not be overlooked. They are just as important when it comes to improving customer care. Each of these secondary processes must be examined carefully and constantly improved through process engineering. Secondary processes that must work in tandem with a quality building program in order to improve customer care include the following:

◆ Human Resource Recruitment and Management

◆ New Product Development

◆ Sales and Marketing

◆ Settlement Processing

◆ Post-Settlement Warranty Service

Each should be a central focus of process engineering to constantly improve the quality of customer care and overall operations. To develop and maintain an effective overall building process, both primary and secondary processes must support one another and adopt the same values and goals.

UNSOLICITED LISTS DURING CONSTRUCTION

On occasion, a purchaser will present the on-site construction manager with a list of items that they see as deficiencies during construction. These lists should be accepted with the provision that the company will not formally respond. Construction is on-going, and such items are routinely corrected during the course of the process and, in most cases, should not be a concern to the buyer. The policy should state that such lists would be accepted, reviewed by the construction manager, and then forwarded to be filed in the permanent lot. In the event that a significant item of concern is included, either the construction manager or a senior production employee must address the issue with the customer and in writing for the record.

THE ORIENTATION PROCESS

One of the most important events in the home building process is the presentation of the new home to the purchaser. It occurs in preparation for settlement and it marks the end of the construction process and the beginning of the post-settlement service process. The specific purpose of the orientation is to: 1) demonstrate the house, 2) provide information related to post-settlement service, and 3) walk the house to inspect finishes. Employees who conduct orientations should be carefully trained for that purpose. The complete agenda should take approximately two hours for a 2,500 sq. ft. home. In those cases where the purchaser has employed a third-party inspector for an inspection upon completion, such inspections should follow the company's formal orientation by at least an hour; this will give the representative of the company an opportunity to complete the orientation before the inspector arrives. In some cases, the company may be willing to combine the final phase of the orientation and the third-party inspection as an accommodation to the customer. The orientation should be almost scripted, include a written summary that acknowledges the discussion of major topics and signature blocks for both the homebuyer and the company representative, and it should be conducted the same way by every employee in order to insure consistency.

THE DEMONSTRATION

The demonstration portion of the orientation should include the following:

1. Operation of kitchen appliances—the demonstration of *key features* that the purchaser might otherwise overlook.
2. Operation of the heating and cooling system—including a discussion of air distribution, standards for cooling performance, thermostat settings, and maintenance requirements. This demonstration should include instructions on the thermostat, changing filters, and the importance of routine maintenance.

3. A detailed discussion of electrical, plumbing, irrigation, security, and other systems that have been provided:

    ◆ Electrical systems should include an examination of the panel box with a discussion of the function of circuit breakers and Ground Fault devices, as well as the location of the main breaker, any exterior receptacles, and any switched receptacles.

    ◆ Plumbing systems should include a discussion of the function of a pressure reducing valve, temperature settings for hot water, the location of cut-off valves (both inside and outside), the location of any saddle valves, and a discussion of a well water system or septic system if provided. The location of the septic tank, the function of a septic system, and its care and maintenance are all critical requirements if a septic system has been provided.

    ◆ Irrigation panel boxes must be demonstrated as well as shutdown and start-up requirements in areas subject to winter conditions.

    ◆ Security systems must be reviewed if they have been provided, including the location of the main panel box, security devices, the battery back-up requirements, the local alarm, and requirements for central monitoring.

    ◆ Central vacuum systems, including installation, equipment, and disposal of debris, should be examined.

4. Other key features of the house, including:

    ◆ Structured wiring; its locations and capacity if it has been provided

    ◆ Conduit provided for future wiring; its location and capacity if it has been provided

    ◆ Smoke detectors, function and maintenance requirements

    ◆ Window features, such as tilt cleaning, the removal of screens, and cleaning suggestions (get these from your professional cleaner).

    ◆ Entrance door keys and security provisions

    ◆ Electronic air cleaners (operation and maintenance)

    ◆ Humidifier (operation and maintenance)

    ◆ A pull-down stair or attic scuttle; location and/or operation

5. Exterior features of the house, including:

    ◆ Storm-water management system; including gutters (and maintenance requirements), splash blocks, grades at the house (and the importance of maintaining these grades), and swales used to direct or divert water. This should also include a discussion of the standards for standing water and water crossing one lot from another.

◆ Landscaping including warranty and watering requirements

◆ Any special maintenance requirements for entrance doors

◆ Exterior repaint requirements (3 to 5 years in most cases)

◆ Winter wavers in those areas where winter weather has delayed final landscaping until Spring

6. Presentation of touch-up kit that includes interior paint and a tube of caulking, at a minimum

POST-SETTLEMENT WARRANTY SERVICE DISCUSSION

The discussion of post-settlement warranty service should probably take place in the kitchen and the representative of the company should have prepared documents to provide the customer that include: 1) letter from the President of the Company, 2) warranty documents, 3) warranty standards, 4) homeowner's maintenance manual, 5) service request forms, and 6) list of trade contractors and phone numbers , 7) list of interior and exterior paint colors, and 8) other material such as reminder notices to water sod and landscaping, discount programs available to purchasers, a business card from the Customer Care Coordinator, and the like. Often, large builders will present this material in a carefully prepared presentation binder to maintain a professional image.

The Presidents (or an appropriate Vice Presidents) letter should congratulate the customer on the impending closing of their new home and formally introduce the customer to the post-settlement service department and its basic policies that will help the purchaser understand the procedures for post-settlement service (see sample). These are the same points that need to be made by the representative conducting the orientation during the post-settlement service discussion.

THE INSPECTION

The purpose of the inspection is to give the customer the opportunity to examine the finishes and acknowledge completion. This should be a room-by-room inspection of walls, ceilings, floors, fixtures, hardware, finished assemblies, appliances, and the like, to note the completion of construction and confirm its acceptance. In the event that an exception is found, it should be placed on a list for correction prior to settlement. This list must become part of the permanent records for each lot; among other things, the form used for orientations will memorializes completion, indicate the condition of the home at the time of presentation, and provide an acknowledgement that a series of important topics have been discussed.

In most cases, the requirement for completion prior to settlement will mean that the orientation will have to be conducted one to two weeks before the anticipated settle-

THE ABC BUILDING COMPANY, INC.
1234 ANYPLACE DRIVE
ROCKVILLE, MD 20854

May 21, 2000

Mr. & Mrs. John Q. Customer
1234 Home Town Drive
Alexandria, VA 22012

Dear John and Mary:

On behalf of all of those who work for *The ABC Building Company,* I would like to thank you for purchasing an ABC home and giving us the opportunity to create this new investment for you. A team of more than seventy-five architects, engineers, code inspectors, construction managers, and tradesmen has participated directly in the construction of your new home. It is a complicated structure of materials, assemblies, and systems designed to provide shelter and support for you and your family. I sincerely hope that we have met your expectations throughout the purchase and production process. We take pride in the homes that we build, and *we are dedicated to the very best in both homebuilding and customer care.*

You have just completed your Homeowner Orientation, which we feel is a significant milestone in the production process. This orientation is designed to help you understand the features and systems in your new home, to become aware of our post-settlement service policy, and to afford you an opportunity to inspect the finishes in your new home. Following the orientation, your Project Manager will have outstanding items on your list completed prior to settlement. Once this list is complete, the obligations of our construction department are terminated and our customer care department takes over; the Project Manager maintains his focus on work-in-process and a Customer Care Representative will then provide any required post-settlement warranty service that you may require. In the event of an emergency, call our customer care department and we will be happy to help in any way that we can. For non-emergency service items, we ask that you prepare a list on the "Post-Settlement Service Request" form that we have provided. These lists should be mailed or faxed to us at sixty (60) days following your settlement and again at eleven (11) months. If it is more convenient for you, this form can be submitted by way of our Internet site at ABCBuildingCompany.com.

We have also enclosed a list of our trade contractors that maintain service departments and we ask that you contact them directly in order to schedule warranty service in those areas. This way, we can minimize your inconvenience and the possibility for confusion by allowing you to set your own schedule directly with them. In the event that a trade contractor is non-responsive or, in the event that you are dissatisfied for any reason, please let us know. You may be assured of our commitment to maintain a high level of customer satisfaction throughout the building process.

We recognize that preparing for the settlement on your new home is a complicated process and can sometimes be overwhelming. You are not only coordinating your orientation and settlement with us, you are also scheduling or coordinating movers, the modification of insurance policies, the transfer of utilities, and much more. We are providing this settlement portfolio in order to give you a single place to compile all of the documents and miscellaneous papers that you will accumulate during your settlement and move. Keep it with you and see how quickly you fill it up.

Again, we sincerely appreciate your confidence and the opportunity to build your new home. Keep in mind that our Customer Care Department is here to serve you. If we can help in any way, regardless of your warranty status, please let us know. It is our hope that everything that we do will continue to preserve the sense of excitement and anticipation that preceded your decision to buy an ABC home. Welcome to your new home and the new community that you have chosen.

Respectfully,

William C. Smith
President

FIGURE 3.1. Customer letter: Introduction to post-settlement service.

ment date. Most home builders will require a re-walk after the work has been completed and prior to the settlement, at which time the customer will be expected to review the noted deficiencies and sign off. No house should be closed with an open list and no home should be presented for an orientation before it has been properly prepared for presentation.

Nothing will do more to destroy a purchaser's goodwill than presenting their new home in an unfinished condition. Delivering a home that has not been properly prepared for presentation is probably the most damaging experience for a homebuyer; it produces a sudden loss of confidence, critical concern for the purchasers investment, concern for the settlement and moving schedule, embarrassment for staff, and general disappointment for everyone involved. It is the most unprofessional mistake that a home builder can make. In my view, this is a violation of a trust and it robs the customer of the natural excitement that should surround the delivery of a new home and the anticipation of moving to a new neighborhood. Very few purchasers will forgive a builder for denying them this opportunity.

In those few cases when a house falls behind schedule in the final phase and does not make the scheduled orientation date, the purchaser should receive a call from the President or a Vice President of the company. A very serious apology is in order, and some very serious assurances must be offered to justify the reschedule of the orientation. In such cases, a dinner-for-two certificate can help ease the disappointment and demonstrate the company's sincerity. Such a disappointment must become the focus of every department in the company and every effort must be made to acknowledge and overcome the disappointment. In a proactive company, it would not be unusual for the President of a Vice President to appear at the rescheduled orientation.

Whole-House Videos

In housing markets with a very high rate of construction litigation, some home builders have contracted with specialists to produce whole-house videos prior to concealment. Such videos are then either given to the customers or archived and maintained by the builder for three to five years. In the event of litigation related to structural conditions or the conditions of the rough-ins prior to drywall, a certified reference video exists. While this may seem extreme, the action is based on the actual awards by local courts in residential construction cases.

EXTRAORDINARY POST-SETTLEMENT SERVICE

The goal of responsible home builders should be to over-service the customer and document it. That is, to provide a level of post-settlement service that is beyond the expectation of the customer and to provide a process that routinely records such extra effort. In order to accomplish this goal, the company must budget for extraordinary service and the effort must be well directed in order to minimize waste and unnecessary expense.

The total cost of warranty service has been estimated by some to be as high as 1 percent of the cost of a new home—or $4,000 for a $400,000 home. The real trick is to look beneath the surface and find the causes of such costly and largely unnecessary service expenditures, and to reduce such costs wherever possible by modifying, either, the design, the construction process, or the service delivery system. In most cases, extraordinary warranty service costs can be traced to one of the following:

1. Inadequate supervision during construction
2. Plan and product deficiencies or product application errors
3. Failure to complete the homeowner orientation list
4. Failure to define warranty standards and set reasonable expectations with the buyer
5. Failure to require the participation of trade contractors and suppliers
6. Failure to enforce reasonable back-charge policies
7. Failure to modify the process as a result of warranty staff feedback
8. Costs related to mismanaging the most difficult customers

Warranty service is provided in accordance with the settlement documents, state and county laws, and within the scope established by the warranty documents provided to the homebuyer at the time of orientation or closing. The warranty standards provided to homeowners upon the execution of their contract and again at their orientation or closing generally serve as guidelines to determine what action is required of the builder as it relates to specific areas of construction. All construction managers and customer care technicians must be knowledgeable about these standards and prepared to discuss them with purchasers and homeowners during the normal course of business. Production Managers, Project Managers, and Superintendents will help set expectations with purchasers during the construction process based largely on these standards, and customer care technicians will use them to help homeowners understand warranty service and homeowner maintenance requirements.

Never refuse to talk to the press. If you have maintained a process of proactive customer care, you have nothing to hide.

- *Discuss the complaint*
- *Describe the process*
- *Present the policies*
- *Present survey results*
- *Review letters of acknowledgement*
- *Open the file for review of service records (only)*
- *Reference this book*

Most successful building companies will go well beyond that which is required by law or as a matter of warranty documents. In order to preserve a reputation for responsive and proactive customer care, the builder and his staff must be prepared to make every reasonable attempt to satisfy homeowners and avoid confrontation wherever practical. In many cases, this will require patience and compromise on the part of the customer care technician. In those cases where a technician feels that a request is absolutely unreasonable and the homeowner is persistent, he or she should obtain a determination from his or her supervisor. In each such case, the technician should be expected to negotiate with the homeowner in an effort to find some acceptable middle ground, but in the event that the homeowner is persistent, others should make the final decision. This will also avoid conflict with the technician at the point of service. In cases where the homeowner is difficult, the technician should work off items on a service request, have them initialed as work progresses, and then deal with items that may be in dispute. That way, in the event that the homeowner refuses to sign off an entire list, at least the items where service has been performed have been documented. With difficult homeowners, service should be denied if they refuse to initial complete items as work progresses; there must be some understanding that the technician is not wasting his or her time.

THE REAL COST OF POST-SETTLEMENT WARRANTY SERVICE

The cost of post-settlement warranty service in a high-volume company with a proactive customer care program should be somewhere between .5% and .75% of the sales price, or between $2,000 and $3,000 per unit for that $400,000 house. Admittedly, this can only occur if there is a well-coordinated effort and everyone embraces the concept of proactive customer care that includes the quality building program. Unfortunately for those companies who must make a transition to a proactive customer care program, the costs can be much higher initially. Costs will usually not exceed 1.25% in a high-volume company, unless there are significant structural failures or major failures in material applications.

SIGN-OFF ACKNOWLEDGMENTS

Most home builders require their customers to sign off on service repairs and corrections resulting from pre-settlement lists and service requests. The purpose of this requirement is to obtain an acknowledgement that the work has been completed and that it is acceptable. Often, the most difficult customers will refuse to make such an acknowledgement. In those cases, the builder has two options: 1) to refuse to move forward with the completion of such items unless the homeowner provides such an acknowledgement, or 2) to complete the work and require that the technician note the homeowner's refusal to sign off on the request for service document, in which case he or she must obtain an inspection and the acknowledgement of a senior production employee indicating a satisfactory completion. In the case of the second option, such a customer may be told that as a matter of policy, the sign-off is merely a courtesy, but not a requirement.

USING CONSULTANTS AND THIRD PARTY INSPECTORS

In cases, in which a customer refuses to accept a reasonable conclusion, it can create an impasse that may result in the loss of goodwill. Often, the employee sees those facts slightly different than the customer because of their knowledge and background in construction and warranty service. This can be a common mistake made by an inexperienced construction manager, service technician, or customer care coordinator, and it should be avoided. In most cases, the solution is as simple as engaging a third-party to make an inspection and render a written opinion for the record. In some cases, the company will have to pay for such an inspection and report, but, in many other instances, third-party inspections can be obtained through vendors at no cost.

Third-party inspectors and consultants can also be used to resolve issues when the course of action is unclear to the company. In some cases, complaints arise out of conditions that are not clearly understood. In those cases, experienced employees will use third-party inspectors and consultants to provide direction and offer support for the customer. In either case, such reports demonstrate an effort to be fair and reasonable, and they provide a documented basis for conclusions that may be challenged later.

AFTER HOURS EMERGENCIES

Some provision must be made for emergency service requirements after normal working hours. In most cases, homeowners receive emergency phone numbers for plumbing and mechanical contractors at the time of their orientation. Unfortunately, other emergencies may occur and the customer may need help. Two effective methods of delivering such after hours service, is by contracting it out to a reliable independent contractor, or by combining an answering service bureau with an on-call technician or construction staff member. If the on-call status is rotated between construction and warranty service personnel on a weekly basis, the individual burden can be kept to a minimum. Those companies that are really committed to a higher level of customer care will offer this service for its homeowners.

POLYGRAPH TESTS

It is not unusual for the toughest customers to unfairly allege theft or misconduct on the part of an employee. Service technicians must be aware of this possibility and protect themselves wherever possible by avoiding one-on-one contact or by taking a second technician on such sensitive service calls. Companies must protect themselves by carefully screening service employees and insuring that they are bonded. Such allegations place the company in a very difficult position, because it must take action based on the possibility that the event may have occurred. It must investigate the circumstances and discuss the conditions with the employee. Such allegations should be investigated and resolved by the most senior employee responsible for customer care. Such complaints should be taken very seriously because they have the potential for considerable legal liability. The employee should be interviewed immediately and very careful questions and answers must be documented for the file. The company must not take either position, but be supportive of both. At the end of the day, the final outcome will be based on facts and nothing more.

Experience indicates that in those cases where an employee is willing to submit to a polygraph test, false accusations often evaporate. It may even be advisable for the employee to volunteer to submit to a polygraph test on the condition that the person alleging the theft or misconduct submits to the same test. Some employers may require service technicians to submit to polygraph tests as a condition of employment, but the potential for a false positive result could have considerable impact on the employee. For this reason, it is probably advisable to deal with this question on a voluntary basis. It may even be advisable for an employee to offer to take a polygraph test under conditions controlled by the company, with the knowledge that it may later be refused under advice of an attorney.

CONFRONTING THE PROBLEM

Every employee must be made aware that confronting issues and complaints from customers is the only way to resolve them and maintain control of the process. Unless employees are proactive in their approach to customer care, they lose the opportunity to demonstrate the extent of their commitment and to minimize the negative effects of such complaints. If an employee suspects that a customer is unhappy, they should call them and discuss the problem before it has had a chance to grow in magnitude. Such actions should be documented; they are indicators of the level of overall commitment on the part of staff that may serve a very valuable purpose down the road. Sometimes, that tough call is the first one that should be placed; by confronting problems quickly and resolving them, the impact of conflict diminishes and frees the employee from unnecessary stress. It also affords an opportunity for the employee to discuss issues when they are prepared and have given it some thought.

In proactive companies, the customer is extended access to everyone. Calls are not screened, senior employees are not exempt, and everyone is prepared to do their part; every employee is expected to respond to the customer and participate in the delivery of customer care. By creating open lines of communication with senior employees, customers come to realize the extent of the company's culture and commitment. It makes a very powerful statement that is unmistakable; the company maintains a customer focus and is dedicated to providing the very highest level of customer care. It also forces everyone to learn to manage the toughest customers, which should be a prerequisite for senior management.

CHAPTER 4

REINFORCE THE COMMITMENT AND UNDERSTAND METHODS OF DISPUTE RESOLUTION

During the normal course of day-to-day activity, the commitment for proactive customer care, and to the process that will deliver it, must be reinforced. It must be reinforced in training programs, in partnership meetings, in new-hire orientations, and, more importantly, in the way that we conduct our businesses. The process must be audited, and individual lot or house files must be reviewed on a random basis to ensure the required documents are finding their way to the correct place. It is only with the knowledge that the process is working, that we can find some measure of comfort with the ordinary risks that are part of dealing with the public in such a complicated industry. The potential for serious conflict with our customers is ongoing and unless we take the necessary steps to protect the company, it faces the possibility of public embarrassment and/or, perhaps, a substantial judgment. Either condition would have a serious impact on employee attitudes and sales (which is the lifeblood of home building companies).

Without the benefit of this process, owners and senior managers cannot be comfortable with the knowledge that their performance is credible and documented. This condition can lead to unnecessary concern for those most difficult customers who are most vocal; who are the same customers who will pursue the owners and senior managers with the intent of discrediting an employee who has acted in good faith. The fear of arbitration, litigation, or bad press will give way to unreasonable compromise with these customers, which will set the stage for low employee morale and even more aggressive behavior from this group. *If the integrity of a proactive customer care process is maintained by every employee, these fears need not be a factor in the benchmark companies that embrace such a process.*

The following are some service policies worth adopting:
- *Never accept a key without executing an acknowledgement that limits the liability of the company*
- *Always screen service technicians carefully and have them acknowledge a drug and alcohol policy, ethics and honesty statements, and dress and behavior requirements*
- *Use door tags with copies to the office for broken appointments, special instructions, etc.*
- *Implement a "knock next door" program requiring technicians who finish early to knock next door and offer limited services while he or she is available*

EMPLOYEES

Employees are the key to maintaining the continuity of the process. They must understand the process and work within it. They must accept their responsibilities both to the customer and within the process. *They must show concern for the documents that must be executed and then delivered safely to the permanent files.* Unless they accept these responsibilities, the chain will be broken and the value of the system will be lost. The process is dependent on every single employee working together to produce the desired result.

Employees must receive a careful orientation on customer care at the time they are hired, they must have access to written policies and descriptions of the process, they must receive ongoing training, they must be held accountable for their contribution, and they must be rewarded for outstanding effort. Each employee will come to find that with a proactive customer care program, they will enjoy a much more confidant position. The unnecessary stress related to the management of every day customer relationships will diminish, they will find a new level of confidence in the performance of the company, the ability to manage the most difficult customers will improve, and their overall performance will yield greater rewards.

TRADE CONTRACTORS AND SUPPLIERS

To minimize costs and reach a higher level of efficiency, trade contractors, suppliers, and other strategic partners must be brought into the process. This can be done in several ways:

◆ Contract Documents; include post-settlement warranty service and customer care topics in their contracts, specifications, and scopes of work

◆ Obtain Commitments; provide information and obtain the commitments of the owners and senior managers of these companies to provide knowledgeable, experienced, and effective service technicians, along with professional, timely, and documented customer service

◆ Reinforce the Need; use partnership meetings to present evaluations of actual performance, areas of concern, and recognition for outstanding performance

◆ Promote Understanding; provide copies of this book to those companies who have the most critical need to understand the process

LETTERS OF ACKNOWLEDGMENT

Letters of acknowledgment and gratitude should be written by an officer of the company and used to encourage and reinforce outstanding performance in the areas of both construction quality and customer care. Such letters should be sent to employees working for trade contractors, suppliers, and other strategic partners (Fig. 4.1). They should be sent to their homes with copies to a permanent file or binder that can be used for display purposes. To carry this program a step further, the home builder should have small plaques engraved with the names, titles, and companies of these outstanding performers and attach them to a display board with a heading that recognizes their effort on behalf of the company. Such an acknowledgment is very powerful, and these employees are deserving of such an acknowledgment.

GIFT CERTIFICATE PROGRAM

When honest mistakes are made, they must be acknowledged as mistakes and some immediate effort must be taken to correct them. This is a requirement for ethical behavior,

---

THE ABC BUILLDING COMPANY, INC.
1234 ANYPLACE DRIVE
ROCKVILLE, MD 20854

November 1, 2002

Mr. James Q. Peterson
5678 Smithfield Court
Arlington, VA 22177

Dear Jim:

I would like to thank you formally for your dedication and effort. Your commitment to maintain high standards in your work helps us deliver a quality product to those families who purchase *ABC* homes. Our work can be frustrating and often difficult. We work in a largely uncontrolled environment, we are dependent on the work of others, coordinating the parts and pieces that we require can be complicated, we are exposed to weather and, during construction we are often too cold or too hot.

Home builders are typically so focused on the negative aspects that affect our production schedules, cycle time, quality standards, and settlement dates, that we tend to forget those who are working hard to help us meet our goals. Your exceptional effort is important to us and I want to be sure that you understand the depth of our commitment to quality. Your name will be engraved on a plate that will be mounted on a plaque in recognition of your effort on our behalf. This plaque will hang in our offices and will memorialize our respect for you and the standards that you set. The success of *The ABC Building Company* is largely built on the effort of hard working, conscientious, people like you.

If there is anything this company or I can do to help you in the future please let me know. You have our respect and it is my hope that others will follow your example.

Respectfully,

William C. Smith
President

C.C. Bill Jones, XYZ Plumbing & Mechanical

FIGURE 4.1. Letter of acknowledgment.

and it sends a very strong signal to staff and others who are involved. In most cases, fair and reasonable people will demonstrate some degree of understanding, provide a reasonable opportunity for correction, and accept an apology. When the company or its employees have made a mistake, some form of documented acknowledgment is entirely appropriate. In such cases, a letter with a dinner gift certificate can provide the perfect acknowledgment (Fig. 4.2).

THE ABC BUILDING COMPANY, INC.
1234 ANYPLACE DRIVE
ROCKVILLE, MD 20854

November 12, 2002

Mr. & Mrs. John Doe
5678 Goodwill Court
Gaithersburg, MD 20870

Dear Bob and Janet:

I would like to apologize for our failure to complete your house in accordance with the schedule that we both anticipated. I recognize the inconvenience and frustration that this has created for you and your family. At a time when you should be excited about the prospect of moving into your new home, you are dealing with disappointment and concern. As you well know, our business is complicated and we are largely at the mercy of others for the labor and material necessary to achieve our delivery target dates. Our goal has been, and will continue to be, one that preserves the excitement and anticipation that should be part of your new home purchase.

We are currently completing the work on your new home and we look forward to presenting it to you on your rescheduled orientation date next week. I will personally see to it that your new home is properly prepared for your orientation. We are currently improving our process in order to provide more reliable information to our purchasers. It is our hope that our performance will improve in this area as our process matures and our trade partnerships improve.

I am enclosing a gift certificate with this letter as a small gesture of our respect for you and to acknowledge your patience and cooperation. I hope that you will enjoy your dinner at the XYZ Restaurant with our complements. I also hope, that by the time you use this certificate, we will have been able to help you feel more comfortable about your new home and your relationship with *The ABC Building Company*. Please be assured that we recognize that customer care is circular and not linear; our relationship with you will continue and we will always be here to provide assistance. Going forward, if I can help you in any way, you can reach me on extension #108 or you may contact Nancy Gooding on extension #115.

Again, we thank you for your patience and understanding.

Respectfully,

William C. Smith
President

Encl.

FIGURE 4.2. Gift certificate letter.

ADVERTISING

Effective reinforcement of a culture dedicated to customer care can result from advertising statements. Carefully crafted statements that are directly linked to the Statements of Purpose or Policies of the company. By placing these statements that essentially promise a higher level of customer care in its advertising, the company puts employees, vendors, and others on notice that it is committed and that it will deliver. Although some home builders will be reluctant to make the promise before an acceptable level has been achieved, experience dictates that such statements will help the company achieve its goals.

A theme that the company provides both a quality building process and proactive customer care should remain secondary, but dominant in every form of advertising. Websites should dedicate considerable space to this theme, printed advertising should repeat it, and videos or CDs should feature it. It should be a reoccurring theme in public statements about the company and owners, investors, lenders, and employees must understand why it makes them different.

METHODS OF DISPUTE RESOLUTION

Every employee must recognize the litigious environment within which we work. Jury awards can be significant and the general belief that home builders make extraordinary profits and are generally not sensitive to the requirements of their purchasers can work against them. Home builders are usually unsuccessful in jury trials. Disputes significantly damage a well-intentioned builder and must not be taken lightly. Home builders and their staff must not fear those few who are unreasonable and have the potential for serious conflict, but they must recognize the sensitive nature of any conflict they encounter.

Dispute resolution is an important part of any proactive customer care program. Disputes are inevitable, and where they are not resolved between the parties in some fair and reasonable compromise, some formal process must be available. Such unresolved disputes are generally submitted for conciliation, mediation, or arbitration, or they become the focus of litigation initiated by the customer as a plaintiff.

CONCILIATION AND MEDIATION

Conciliation and *mediation* are non-binding processes that rely on a third party, such as an architect, engineer, or well-qualified construction inspector to render an opinion. Because it is a non-binding process, this method of dispute resolution is almost never recommended except in those few cases when you are convinced that the complaining party is truly a fair and reasonable person.

ARBITRATION

Arbitration is a non-judicial procedure, in which a neutral third party, selected by both sides, renders either binding or non-binding decision. It is most advisable to resolve

Never offer to refund a deposit as a matter of normal exchange with a difficult customer. This is an insult and, in most cases, does not play well in court. Only the most senior employee can make this suggestion, and it should only be used in the most difficult cases. It should be presented as a final option available to the purchaser upon his or her written request.

disputes by means of arbitration wherever possible. Costs are reasonable, it occurs more quickly than litigation, and a jury is not involved. Many home builders are inserting language in contracts for the sale of homes, which requires *binding* arbitration as a means of resolving disputes. If indeed, a home builder has maintained a proactive process and if his primary concern is for his reputation and the good will of others, he has nothing to fear from arbitration. Unless it is an unusual case, an attorney should not represent the home builder in an arbitration cases. An attorney presents a more difficult situation for the arbitrator, and the builder or his senior representative should be able to present a well-documented effort by the company to over-service the customer, as well as a fair and reasonable attempt to avoid the need for such arbitration.

The creation of an effective case for arbitration (or any formal proceeding designed to resolve a dispute) begins long before the actual dispute develops. The strongest case a builder can present is one in which he has been professional with respect to his responsibilities: that is, he has well written contracts, warranties, and specifications; he has documented efforts to resolve the dispute fairly; and, in the case of a warranty service complaint, he must be able to demonstrate that he has gone well beyond what is fair and reasonable in an effort to resolve the dispute and satisfy the home owner. Written service requests, inspection reports, and photographs of field conditions should all be produced as a normal matter of conducting business.

In most cases, it takes six weeks or more to schedule an arbitration case and perhaps another six weeks for the decision to be rendered. In those instances where a homeowner is abusive and threatening, it can serve to remove the open hostility and defer action until the case is heard and a decision has been rendered. In those instances where arbitration is not a legal requirement, it becomes an art to get a difficult customer to agree to an arbitration. In all cases, the offer of arbitration should be made in writing with a copy to the file; this will document the attempt to be fair and reasonable.

LITIGATION

Litigation is a legal process that uses the courts to resolve questions of law in civil cases. The stages of this procedure are: 1) pleadings, 2) pretrial, 3) trial, 4) appeal, and 5) enforcement. Home builders should avoid litigation at all reasonable costs. Litigation is expensive; it is time consuming; it creates ill will; and it also becomes a matter of public record. If you are a defendant, try to find a compromise position that will settle the dispute, and if you are the plaintiff and initiate the litigation, it should only occur after considerable effort has been made and documented to resolve matters outside of court. A building professional should not fear litigation, but he or she must be realistic about its potential outcome; the outcome of a trial is seldom predictable, and attorneys are trained to argue effectively on either side. In the event that litigation is unavoidable, the builder should use an experienced trial attorney with a reputation for success.

In all cases, the potential for success favors the home builder with a proactive customer care program. Efforts to satisfy the customer are well documented and the company has a history of fair and reasonable behavior. Although home builders have not generally faired well in jury trials historically, the benefits of a proactive process are considerable. It would not be unusual for an attorney to refuse to argue a case where the home builder can document his or her efforts to be fair and reasonable, particularly in warranty service cases. I have personally experienced this in two instances over a thirty-five year career and in one case, the plaintiff's attorney actually gave me advice that helped me protect myself. That is not to say that a home builder who has failed to properly coordinate field construction with plans, specifications, and scopes of work, or these documents with sales specifications, feature sheets, or option descriptions used for sales, would not be hard pressed to defend his or her position. In fact, in these cases, it often comes to the question of what a reasonable person might assume.

Everyone in the company must be aware of the right of a litigant to require answers to interrogatories or questions, the production of specific documents, and depositions of individuals during the pretrial phase of litigation. Any information placed in a file or otherwise maintained by the company must be relevant and professional in nature. If logs or summaries of conditions are maintained, they must be carefully written in order to avoid a negative impact in the event of litigation. If each employee conducts business in accordance with the suggestions contained in this book and applies reasonable business practice, the possibility of a negative impact would be considerably reduced.

Never assume that you can intimidate a homeowner by refusing to respond or provide a fair and reasonable resolve to their complaints. Today, everyone is knowledgeable about his or her rights and, more importantly, he or she knows how to assert them. You are obligated to respond and to respond with a fair and reasonable solution.

In a proactive company, the need for formal dispute resolution should be minimal. Most disputes will be resolved between the parties based on some fair and reasonable compromise. In those cases where others must resolve disputes, builders should avoid litigation wherever possible; as it has been pointed out, it is costly, time consuming, and often has a negative outcome. For this reason, home builders should insert an arbitration clause in their sales contracts in states where it is appropriate. Such clauses require that disputes be resolved by arbitration rather than litigation; mandatory, binding arbitration is less costly, timelier, and avoids the possible prejudice of a jury.

CREATING DEFENSE

How then, do we prepare for these formal methods of dispute resolution? The very first requirement is for the company to establish a reputation for being fair and reasonable. Although mistakes are made with very serious legal consequences, most disputes with homeowners are without merit in companies with a proactive customer care program; they typically result from the unfair and unreasonable demands of your most difficult customers. Fortunately, the process will provide the builder with the *documents required* to defend his or her position. In most arbitration hearings, a defense will only require a well-written summary with supporting documents to defend a position. The file should have been prepared in the normal course of business and it should have been reviewed and organized by the senior management employee with oversight responsibility for these difficult customers. Litigation on the other hand would be much more complicated and costly.

The most difficult part of pretrial preparation producing documents and answering questions posed by the plaintiff. Employees must be very careful when placing documents in a file; you must maintain the documents necessary for the defense of your position, but nothing should be retained that might be used against you by a clever attorney who might be tempted to twist the facts. If the integrity of the process has been maintained, company records and every individual lot files should contain the following documents.

Documents Related to the Process

◆ Statements of purpose; taken from employee manuals, policy manuals, and institutional advertising

◆ Policy and procedures; relevant policy statements and written descriptions of procedures

◆ Descriptions of the Quality Building Program; process descriptions provided in standard memo or policy format that describe the Quality Building Program

◆ Descriptions of the Post-Settlement Warranty Service Program; process descriptions provided in standard memo or policy format that describe the Post-Settlement Warranty Service Program

◆ Warranty and warranty standards documents; standard descriptions of the homeowner warranty and the warranty standards, that are used to determine responsibility, given to the customer both at the time of contract and again at settlement

Case-Specific Documents

◆ Contract documents; executed contracts, addenda, and change orders on standardized forms, that have been prepared and approved by an attorney

◆ Footing certification; evidence that reasonable care has been taken with regard to soil conditions and the foundation of the structure

◆ Routine correspondence; standard form letters that have resulted from a *letter-writing campaign* designed to provide critical information necessary to help the customer, which also documents both the intent of the company and its efforts to inform its customers

◆ Construction meeting forms; standard forms that validate a willingness to involve the customer in the construction process, document critical topics of discussion, and memorialize the *pre-construction meeting* and the *pre-drywall walk*

◆ Orientation form; a standard form that documents the critical topics of discussion during the pre-settlement demonstration, the condition of the home at closing, and the customers satisfaction *prior to settlement*

◆ Service request forms; standard forms submitted by the homeowner and required for post-settlement warranty service, that contain notations by the service technician and other employees, as well as acknowledgements by the homeowner

◆ Third-party inspection reports; includes reports by others that have been initiated by the company during construction in order to document critical conditions, or after settlement in order to document conditions as they relate to warranty service

◆ Formal internal inspections; formal inspections generally memorialized by a formal written report with photographs, that are made by a senior manager as a result of a request by the customer, or to document specific conditions

◆ Position letters; critical correspondence that has been written by the company to document its position for both the homeowner and for the record. These are often proactive letters used *to establish the exact conditions of communications on sensitive issues* written with the knowledge that they may become a critical focus during a formal dispute resolution process in the future.

◆ Door hangers; standard notation forms used by staff that document efforts to provide service, instructions to customers, general information, or to memorialize broken appointments

Performance Validation

◆ Survey results; surveys are probably the most telling evidence of the effectiveness of any customer care program because they demonstrate a very serious effort on the part of the company and it memorializes the effectiveness of an overall process designed to provide customer care

◆ Letters of acknowledgment; letters of referral and acknowledgment written by customers that serve to validate the commitment to customer care that are very carefully maintained in a file and displayed by the company

◆ Public relations program; an organized program designed to insure a history of ethical behavior that includes contributions, donations, staff activities, and other efforts to improve the quality of life in the community

Companies with such a well-organized process become an attorney's dream and the answer to an investor's prayers.

PART III THE EXECUTION

Implementing a proactive customer care program requires the same advanced planning and follow-up as is required to implement a business plan. It begins with the development of strategic and financial plans; the creation of statements of purpose, policies, and process descriptions; the establishment of the proper culture; and the creation of a method for measuring results. Until now, this book has focused on the strategies, the statements of purpose, policies, the overall process, the culture, and the need for measuring results. We have talked about the need for proactive customer care; we have discussed the need for direction, which is established by written statements of purpose and policy; we discussed the need for well-coordinated sales documents and displays and discussed a quality building program, an effective orientation, and an effective Post-Settlement Service Program; we have discussed the need to create a culture that reinforces the goals and objectives; and, we have discussed methods of measuring results. Now, working backward, let's look at the strategy that brought us to this process and the financial considerations for its implementation.

CHAPTER 5

MAINTAIN A WELL-DEFINED PROCESS AND DOCUMENT CUSTOMER SATISFACTION

STRATEGIES AND FINANCIAL PLANS

*T*he strategy is to create an effective delivery system for proactive customer care that involves the entire company and provides a much higher level of customer service for both our homebuyers and homeowners; a system or process that focuses attention on the eighty percent of our purchasers—those who respond favorably to extra effort. This process also effectively manages our most difficult customers. A process that maintains a customer focus, insures ethical behavior, and avoids the conflicts and disputes that create considerable risk for home builders. Such a strategy should be clearly identified in the company's business plan and considerable effort should be taken to describe the process in detail. This will have the effect of: 1) creating the commitment for the company and establishing the guidelines for staff, 2) providing a higher level of comfort and security for investors, lenders, strategic partners, and others who review such plans in terms of risk management, and 3) ensuring acceptance by senior staff as the plan is reviewed, debated, and adopted.

BUDGETS

Most home builders set up reserves for post-settlement service based on current budgets together with an analysis of industry averages, current experience, and historical facts. In most cases, these reserves will be heavy in order to insure adequacy. As service work is undertaken, the costs are charged back against the established service reserves. Adjustments are made to the reserves from time-to-time throughout the life of projects; as projects and service budgets are routinely reviewed and updated in preparation for a new "roll up" of the business plan, which typically occurs at year-end with a reforecast at mid-year.

As discussed earlier, the responsibility for post-settlement warranty service should rest with the Director or Vice President of Production. It should be his or her responsibility to prepare the Post-Settlement Service Budget for submission, approval, and ultimate inclusion in the company's business plan. These worksheets ensure that the company will be able to operate within the established reserves. The budget should be a compilation of both hard and soft costs spread over every project in process with a month-to-month distribution of costs. Costs should include both administrative and direct labor chargeable to the projects, but the administrative costs associated with the Director or Vice President of Production should be excluded; they are part of the overall costs carried in the General and Administrative Budget for the company. In most cases, direct labor will be applied to new projects two months following the delivery of the first unit and will continue for eleven months following the substantial completion and last home delivered on the project. Service requirements generally diminish following the routine sixty-day service and this should be taken into account in the final eleven months of a completed project.

In most cases, a single experienced technician can manage routine service on approximately fifty to sixty-five homes depending on the velocity of the project, the complexity of the product, the level of participation by trade contractors, and the quality of fit and finish at delivery. In a system in which routine service occurs at 60 days and again at 11 months, each new home requires two scheduled visits for routine service in addition to the service requests that occur outside of the normal process. If the project is closing fifteen units per month, it will produce a service requirement that is too great for one technician; if trade contractors are responsive and support the service effort, the requirement favors more management and less hands-on work; and, if the quality of fit and finish is high, the need for point-up and touch-up is diminished, which will improve the productivity of service technicians. Experience tells us that the key to the productivity of service technicians is process control and compensation.

In companies with a volume of 300 units or less per year, skilled service technicians who are capable of both making repairs and managing the process should be employed. This eliminates the need for a service manager or director of service, a function of oversight and coordination that can be provided by the Director or Vice President of Production and the Customer Care Coordinator. In companies with a volume greater than three hundred units per year, or a company delivering more than one hundred and fifty units per year with a considerable backlog of poorly serviced customers, a Director of Customer Care is probably a requirement; in this instance, he or she should report to the Vice President of Production or a Vice President of Operations; at this level, it becomes necessary to remove the responsibility for day-to-day post-settlement service from the production department.

The most important ingredient for outstanding post-settlement service is the service technician. Home builders should use more technicians and eliminate the unnecessary cost of middle management wherever possible. To accomplish this goal, technicians must *not* make appointments to review work unless it is absolutely necessary. They should be prepared to provide the required service indicated on the homeowners Service Request Form; this will eliminate a non-productive appointment with the homeowner, avoid confrontation before work has been undertaken in those cases in which unreasonable demands have been made, and it will help the technician protect his or her time. Using technicians in this fashion requires management to closely monitor both daily schedules and lists in order to measure productivity. Unless technicians can see that management is measuring productivity and rewarding extra effort, productivity will not reach the level that it might otherwise.

BUDGETS AND DOCUMENTS

The following budgets and documents are provided as examples of forms that may be used to support a proactive customer care program. The author has used The ABC Building Company, Inc. as an example for illustration purposes only; neither the company nor the individuals referred to in these documents exist in fact.

Budgets

The sample budget includes a Life-of-Project Spreadsheet for a single project (one of five projects in process), together with a Post-Settlement Service Summary Sheet (Figs. 5.1 and 5.2). In a typical company, these financial documents would be used as worksheets for evaluation before a rolled-up departmental financial plans and worksheets that become a significant part the business plan for a home building company.

Documents

The attached sample documents include the following standard forms:

◆ Pre-Construction Meeting Form (Fig. 5.3)

◆ Quality Assurance Checklist (Fig. 5.4)

◆ Pre-Drywall Walk Form (Fig. 5.5)

◆ Pre-Settlement Orientation Form (Fig. 5.6)

◆ Post-Settlement Service Request Form (Fig. 5.7)

◆ Service Work Order Form (Fig. 5.8)

◆ Field Inspection Report Policy (Fig. 5.9)

PROACTIVE DOCUMENTATION

An important part of providing proactive customer care and protecting the interests of the company are letters written by an officer of the company to its customers. Such letters are examples of calculated action taken with the express intent of documenting either the behavior of a difficult customer, the position of the company, or the resolution to a problem that may become an issue at some point in the future.

The letter to Mr. Lee (Fig. 5.10) represents an action designed to document unacceptable behavior and set the stage for a termination letter 18 months later. The customer has a long history of complaints, unreasonable behavior, and threats. The President of ABC has been managing this file since the settlement occurred in July, and the file documents are both complete and well organized.

The letter to Mrs. Jones (Fig. 5.11) represents an action designed to document the company's position relating to an ongoing cooling issue. The original complaint surfaced as

WARRANTY-SERVICE PROJECT COST PROJECTIONS
ABC BUILDING COMPANY, INC.
FOR FIVE YEARS BEGINNING JANUARY, 2002

Date: 10/01/2002

Description	Jan-02	Feb-02	Mar-02	Apr-02	May-02	Jun-02	Jul-02	Aug-02	Sep-02	Oct-02	Nov-02	Dec-02	Total
					ACTUAL								
POTOMAC COMMONS													
Settlements	1	1	2	2	1	1	3	3	3	3	2	2	24
Warranty Costs													
Service Technician	2,480	2,480	2,480	2,480	2,480	2,480	2,480	2,480	2,480	2,520	2,520	2,520	29,880
Miscellaneous Labor	-	-	-	-	-	-	-	-	-	-	-	-	-
Truck Expense	250	250	250	250	250	250	250	250	250	250	250	250	3,000
Material	148	96	44	83	51	59	94	43	28	75	75	75	871
Tools & Equipment	62	27	42	113	34	28	69	53	57	100	100	100	785
Other	47	31	47	22	61	55	61	41	57	50	50	50	572
Total Warranty Costs	2,987	2,884	2,863	2,948	2,876	2,872	2,954	2,867	2,872	2,995	2,995	2,995	35,108
BAYWOOD STATION													
Settlements	3	3	3	3	3	3	3	3	3	3	3	3	36
Warranty Costs													
Service Technician	2,480	2,480	2,480	2,480	2,480	2,480	2,480	2,480	2,480	2,520	2,520	2,520	29,880
Miscellaneous Labor	-	-	-	-	-	-	-	-	-	-	-	-	-
Truck Expense	250	250	250	250	250	250	250	250	250	250	250	250	3,000
Material	24	63	51	87	54	66	31	82	55	75	75	75	738
Tools & Equipment	-	-	-	95	95	95	95	95	95	100	100	100	870
Other	14	23	47	22	61	41	27	14	19	50	50	50	418
Total Warranty Costs	2,768	2,816	2,828	2,934	2,940	2,932	2,883	2,921	2,899	2,995	2,995	2,995	34,906
FAIRFAX PARK													
Settlements							3	3	2	2	3	2	15
Warranty Costs													
Service Technician	-	-	-	-	-	-	2,250	3,504	3,504	2,520	2,520	2,520	16,818
Miscellaneous Labor	-	-	-	-	-	-	-	-	-	-	-	-	-
Truck Expense	-	-	-	-	-	-	250	250	250	250	250	250	1,500
Material	-	-	-	-	-	-	88	65	43	75	75	75	421
Tools & Equipment	-	-	-	-	-	-	47	92	29	100	100	100	468
Other	-	-	-	-	-	-	81	66	71	50	50	50	368
Total Warranty Costs	-	-	-	-	-	-	2,716	3,977	3,897	2,995	2,995	2,995	19,575
STONEHENGE													
Settlements									1	3	3	3	10
Warranty Costs													
Service Technician	-	-	-	-	-	-	-	-	3,504	2,520	2,520	2,520	30,318
Miscellaneous Labor	-	-	-	-	-	-	-	-	-	-	-	-	6,720
Truck Expense	-	-	-	-	-	-	-	-	250	250	250	250	900
Material	-	-	-	-	-	-	-	-	67	75	75	75	2,386
Tools & Equipment	-	-	-	-	-	-	-	-	44	100	100	100	870
Other	-	-	-	-	-	-	-	-	19	50	50	50	418
Total Warranty Costs	-	-	-	-	-	-	-	-	3,884	2,995	2,995	2,995	41,612
GRUBBT THICKET													
Settlements													
Warranty Costs													
Service Technician	-	-	-	-	-	-	-	-	-	-	-	-	-
Miscellaneous Labor	-	-	-	-	-	-	-	-	-	-	-	-	-
Truck Expense	-	-	-	-	-	-	-	-	-	-	-	-	-
Material	-	-	-	-	-	-	-	-	-	-	-	-	-
Tools & Equipment	-	-	-	-	-	-	-	-	-	-	-	-	-
Other	-	-	-	-	-	-	-	-	-	-	-	-	-
Total Warranty Costs	-	-	-	-	-	-	-	-	-	-	-	-	-

FIGURE 5.1A. Post-Settlement service summary sheet and cost projections.

Description	Jan-03	Feb-03	Mar-03	Apr-03	May-03	Jun-03	Jul-03	Aug-03	Sep-03	Oct-03	Nov-03	Dec-03	Total
POTOMAC COMMONS													
Settlements	1	1	3	3	1	1	3	3	4	4	4	2	30
Warranty Costs													
Service Technician	2,100	4,000	4,000	4,000	4,000	4,000	4,000	4,000	4,000	4,000	4,000	4,000	46,100
Miscellaneous Labor	1,500	1,500	1,500	1,500	1,500	1,500	1,500	1,500	1,500	1,500	1,500	1,500	18,000
Truck Expense	275	275	275	275	275	275	275	275	275	275	275	275	3,300
Material	80	80	80	80	80	80	80	80	80	80	80	80	960
Tools & Equipment	110	110	110	110	110	110	110	110	110	110	110	110	1,320
Other	60	60	60	60	60	60	60	60	60	60	60	60	720
Total Warranty Costs	4,125	6,025	6,025	6,025	6,025	6,025	6,025	6,025	6,025	6,025	6,025	6,025	70,400
BAYWOOD STATION													
Settlements	2	3	3	4	4	4	3	3	4	4	3	3	40
Warranty Costs													
Service Technician	2,100	4,000	4,000	4,000	4,000	4,000	4,000	4,000	4,000	4,000	4,000	4,000	46,100
Miscellaneous Labor	1,500	1,500	1,500	1,500	1,500	1,500	1,500	1,500	1,500	1,500	1,500	1,500	18,000
Truck Expense	275	275	275	275	275	275	275	275	275	275	275	275	3,300
Material	80	80	80	80	80	80	80	80	80	80	80	80	960
Tools & Equipment	110	110	110	110	110	110	110	110	110	110	110	110	1,320
Other	60	60	60	60	60	60	60	60	60	60	60	60	720
Total Warranty Costs	4,125	6,025	6,025	6,025	6,025	6,025	6,025	6,025	6,025	6,025	6,025	6,025	70,400
FAIRFAX PARK													
Settlements	1	1	3	3	1	1	4	4	4	4	2	2	30
Warranty Costs													
Service Technician	2,100	4,000	4,000	4,000	4,000	4,000	4,000	4,000	4,000	4,000	4,000	4,000	46,100
Miscellaneous Labor	1,500	1,500	1,500	1,500	1,500	1,500	1,500	1,500	1,500	1,500	1,500	1,500	18,000
Truck Expense	275	275	275	275	275	275	275	275	275	275	275	275	3,300
Material	80	80	80	80	80	80	80	80	80	80	80	80	960
Tools & Equipment	110	110	110	110	110	110	110	110	110	110	110	110	1,320
Other	60	60	60	60	60	60	60	60	60	60	60	60	720
Total Warranty Costs	4,125	6,025	6,025	6,025	6,025	6,025	6,025	6,025	6,025	6,025	6,025	6,025	70,400
STONEHENGE													
Settlements	2	2	2	2	2	2	2	2	2	2	2	2	24
Warranty Costs													
Service Technician	2,100	4,000	4,000	4,000	4,000	4,000	4,000	4,000	4,000	4,000	4,000	4,000	46,100
Miscellaneous Labor	1,500	1,500	1,500	1,500	1,500	1,500	1,500	1,500	1,500	1,500	1,500	1,500	18,000
Truck Expense	275	275	275	275	275	275	275	275	275	275	275	275	3,300
Material	80	80	80	80	80	80	80	80	80	80	80	80	960
Tools & Equipment	110	110	110	110	110	110	110	110	110	110	110	110	1,320
Other	60	60	60	60	60	60	60	60	60	60	60	60	720
Total Warranty Costs	4,125	6,025	6,025	6,025	6,025	6,025	6,025	6,025	6,025	6,025	6,025	6,025	70,400
GRUBBT THICKET													
Settlements	-	-	-	-	-	-	-	2	2	2	2	2	10
Warranty Costs													
Service Technician	-	-	-	-	-	-	-	4,000	4,000	4,000	4,000	4,000	20,000
Miscellaneous Labor	-	-	-	-	-	-	-	1,500	1,500	1,500	1,500	1,500	7,500
Truck Expense	-	-	-	-	-	-	-	275	275	275	275	275	1,375
Material	-	-	-	-	-	-	-	80	80	80	80	80	400
Tools & Equipment	-	-	-	-	-	-	-	110	110	110	110	110	550
Other	-	-	-	-	-	-	-	60	60	60	60	60	300
Total Warranty Costs	-	-	-	-	-	-	-	6,025	6,025	6,025	6,025	6,025	30,125

FIGURE 5.1B. Post-Settlement service summary sheet and cost projections.

Description	Jan-04	Feb-04	Mar-04	Apr-04	May-04	Jun-04	Jul-04	Aug-04	Sep-04	Oct-04	Nov-04	Dec-04	Total
POTOMAC COMMONS													
Settlements	2	2	3	3	1	1	1	4	4	4	4	4	36
Warranty Costs													
Service Technician	6,000	6,000	6,000	6,000	6,000	6,000	6,000	6,000	6,000	6,000	6,000	6,000	72,000
Miscellaneous Labor	1,700	1,700	1,700	1,700	1,700	1,700	1,700	1,700	1,700	1,700	1,700	1,700	20,400
Truck Expense	300	300	300	300	300	300	300	300	300	300	300	300	3,600
Material	85	85	85	85	85	85	85	85	85	85	85	85	1,020
Tools & Equipment	120	120	120	120	120	120	120	120	120	120	120	120	1,440
Other	70	70	70	70	70	70	70	70	70	70	70	70	840
Total Warranty Costs	8,275	8,275	8,275	8,275	8,275	8,275	8,275	8,275	8,275	8,275	8,275	8,275	99,300
BAYWOOD STATION													
Settlements	4	4	4	4	4	4	4	4	4	4	4	4	48
Warranty Costs													
Service Technician	6,000	6,000	6,000	6,000	6,000	6,000	6,000	6,000	6,000	6,000	6,000	6,000	72,000
Miscellaneous Labor	1,700	1,700	1,700	1,700	1,700	1,700	1,700	1,700	1,700	1,700	1,700	1,700	20,400
Truck Expense	300	300	300	300	300	300	300	300	300	300	300	300	3,600
Material	85	85	85	85	85	85	85	85	85	85	85	85	1,020
Tools & Equipment	120	120	120	120	120	120	120	120	120	120	120	120	1,440
Other	70	70	70	70	70	70	70	70	70	70	70	70	840
Total Warranty Costs	8,275	8,275	8,275	8,275	8,275	8,275	8,275	8,275	8,275	8,275	8,275	8,275	99,300
FAIRFAX PARK													
Settlements	2	2	3	3	1	1	4	4	4	4	4	4	36
Warranty Costs													
Service Technician	6,000	6,000	6,000	6,000	6,000	6,000	6,000	6,000	6,000	6,000	6,000	6,000	72,000
Miscellaneous Labor	1,700	1,700	1,700	1,700	1,700	1,700	1,700	1,700	1,700	1,700	1,700	1,700	20,400
Truck Expense	300	300	300	300	300	300	300	300	300	300	300	300	3,600
Material	85	85	85	85	85	85	85	85	85	85	85	85	1,020
Tools & Equipment	120	120	120	120	120	120	120	120	120	120	120	120	1,440
Other	70	70	70	70	70	70	70	70	70	70	70	70	840
Total Warranty Costs	8,275	8,275	8,275	8,275	8,275	8,275	8,275	8,275	8,275	8,275	8,275	8,275	99,300
STONEHENGE													
Settlements	3	3	3	3	1	2	3	4	4	4	4	3	36
Warranty Costs													
Service Technician	6,000	6,000	6,000	6,000	6,000	6,000	6,000	6,000	6,000	6,000	6,000	6,000	72,000
Miscellaneous Labor	1,700	1,700	1,700	1,700	1,700	1,700	1,700	1,700	1,700	1,700	1,700	1,700	28,800
Truck Expense	300	300	300	300	300	300	300	300	300	300	300	300	4,320
Material	85	85	85	85	85	85	85	85	85	85	85	85	1,020
Tools & Equipment	120	120	120	120	120	120	120	120	120	120	120	120	1,440
Other	70	70	70	70	70	70	70	70	70	70	70	70	840
Total Warranty Costs	8,275	8,275	8,275	8,275	8,275	8,275	8,275	8,275	8,275	8,275	8,275	8,275	108,420
GRUBBT THICKET													
Settlements	1	2	3	3	1	1	3	4	4	3	3	2	30
Warranty Costs													
Service Technician	6,000	6,000	6,000	6,000	6,000	6,000	6,000	6,000	6,000	6,000	6,000	6,000	72,000
Miscellaneous Labor	1,700	1,700	1,700	1,700	1,700	1,700	1,700	1,700	1,700	1,700	1,700	1,700	20,400
Truck Expense	300	300	300	300	300	300	300	300	300	300	300	300	3,600
Material	85	85	85	85	85	85	85	85	85	85	85	85	1,020
Tools & Equipment	120	120	120	120	120	120	120	120	120	120	120	120	1,440
Other	70	70	70	70	70	70	70	70	70	70	70	70	840
Total Warranty Costs	8,275	8,275	8,275	8,275	8,275	8,275	8,275	8,275	8,275	8,275	8,275	8,275	99,300

FIGURE 5.1C. Post-Settlement service summary sheet and cost projections.

Description	Jan-05	Feb-05	Mar-05	Apr-05	May-05	Jun-05	Jul-05	Aug-05	Sep-05	Oct-05	Nov-05	Dec-05	Total
POTOMAC COMMONS													
Settlements	4	5	5	6		3	6	6	7	7	7	7	63
Warranty Costs													
Service Technician	8,000	8,000	8,000	8,000	8,000	8,000	8,000	8,000	8,000	8,000	8,000	8,000	96,000
Miscellaneous Labor	1,900	1,900	1,900	1,900	1,900	1,900	1,900	1,900	1,900	1,900	1,900	1,900	22,800
Truck Expense	325	325	325	325	325	325	325	325	325	325	325	325	3,900
Material	90	90	90	90	90	90	90	90	90	90	90	90	1,080
Tools & Equipment	130	130	130	130	130	130	130	130	130	130	130	130	1,560
Other	80	80	80	80	80	80	80	80	80	80	80	80	960
Total Warranty Costs	10,525	10,525	10,525	10,525	10,525	10,525	10,525	10,525	10,525	10,525	10,525	10,525	126,300
BAYWOOD STATION													
Settlements	5	4	5	5		4	4	5	6	6	4	3	51
Warranty Costs													
Service Technician	8,000	8,000	8,000	8,000	8,000	8,000	8,000	8,000	8,000	8,000	8,000	8,000	96,000
Miscellaneous Labor	1,900	1,900	1,900	1,900	1,900	1,900	1,900	1,900	1,900	1,900	1,900	1,900	22,800
Truck Expense	325	325	325	325	325	325	325	325	325	325	325	325	3,900
Material	90	90	90	90	90	90	90	90	90	90	90	90	1,080
Tools & Equipment	130	130	130	130	130	130	130	130	130	130	130	130	1,560
Other	80	80	80	80	80	80	80	80	80	80	80	80	960
Total Warranty Costs	10,525	10,525	10,525	10,525	10,525	10,525	10,525	10,525	10,525	10,525	10,525	10,525	126,300
FAIRFAX PARK													
Settlements	4	5	5	6		3	6	6	7	7	7	7	63
Warranty Costs													
Service Technician	8,000	8,000	8,000	8,000	8,000	8,000	8,000	8,000	8,000	8,000	8,000	8,000	96,000
Miscellaneous Labor	1,900	1,900	1,900	1,900	1,900	1,900	1,900	1,900	1,900	1,900	1,900	1,900	22,800
Truck Expense	325	325	325	325	325	325	325	325	325	325	325	325	3,900
Material	90	90	90	90	90	90	90	90	90	90	90	90	1,080
Tools & Equipment	130	130	130	130	130	130	130	130	130	130	130	130	1,560
Other	80	80	80	80	80	80	80	80	80	80	80	80	960
Total Warranty Costs	10,525	10,525	10,525	10,525	10,525	10,525	10,525	10,525	10,525	10,525	10,525	10,525	126,300
STONEHENGE													
Settlements	4	3	4	4		3	4	4	2	3	3	2	36
Warranty Costs													
Service Technician	8,000	8,000	8,000	8,000	8,000	8,000	8,000	8,000	8,000	8,000	8,000	8,000	96,000
Miscellaneous Labor	1,900	1,900	1,900	1,900	1,900	1,900	1,900	1,900	1,900	1,900	1,900	1,900	31,200
Truck Expense	325	325	325	325	325	325	325	325	325	325	325	325	31,200
Material	90	90	90	90	90	90	90	90	90	90	90	90	1,080
Tools & Equipment	130	130	130	130	130	130	130	130	130	130	130	130	1,560
Other	80	80	80	80	80	80	80	80	80	80	80	80	960
Total Warranty Costs	10,525	10,525	10,525	10,525	10,525	10,525	10,525	10,525	10,525	10,525	10,525	10,525	162,000
GRUBBT THICKET													
Settlements	4	5	5	6		3	6	6	7	7	7	7	63
Warranty Costs													
Service Technician	8,000	8,000	8,000	8,000	8,000	8,000	8,000	8,000	8,000	8,000	8,000	8,000	96,000
Miscellaneous Labor	1,900	1,900	1,900	1,900	1,900	1,900	1,900	1,900	1,900	1,900	1,900	1,900	22,800
Truck Expense	325	325	325	325	325	325	325	325	325	325	325	325	3,900
Material	90	90	90	90	90	90	90	90	90	90	90	90	1,080
Tools & Equipment	130	130	130	130	130	130	130	130	130	130	130	130	1,560
Other	80	80	80	80	80	80	80	80	80	80	80	80	960
Total Warranty Costs	10,525	10,525	10,525	10,525	10,525	10,525	10,525	10,525	10,525	10,525	10,525	10,525	126,300

FIGURE 5.1D. Post-Settlement service summary sheet and cost projections.

Description	Jan-06	Feb-06	Mar-06	Apr-06	May-06	Jun-06	Jul-06	Aug-06	Sep-06	Oct-06	Nov-06	Dec-06	Total	Grnd Total
POTOMAC COMMONS														217
Settlements	4	5	6	6	3	6	7	5	7	5	6	4	64	
Warranty Costs														
Service Technician	8,200	8,200	8,200	8,200	8,200	8,200	8,200	8,200	8,200	8,200	8,200	8,200	98,400	342,380
Miscellaneous Labor	2,100	2,100	2,100	2,100	2,100	2,100	2,100	2,100	2,100	2,100	2,100	2,100	25,200	86,400
Truck Expense	350	350	350	350	350	350	350	350	350	350	350	350	4,200	18,000
Material	95	95	95	95	95	95	95	95	95	95	95	95	1,140	5,071
Tools & Equipment	140	140	140	140	140	140	140	140	140	140	140	140	1,680	6,785
Other	90	90	90	90	90	90	90	90	90	90	90	90	1,080	4,172
Total Warranty Costs	10,975	10,975	10,975	10,975	10,975	10,975	10,975	10,975	10,975	10,975	10,975	10,975	131,700	462,808
BAYWOOD STATION														210
Settlements	5	5	6	4	5	5	5						35	
Warranty Costs														
Service Technician	8,200	8,200	8,200	8,200	8,200	8,200	8,200	8,200	8,200	-	-	-	73,800	317,780
Miscellaneous Labor	2,100	2,100	2,100	2,100	2,100	2,100	2,100	2,100	-	-	-	-	16,800	78,000
Truck Expense	350	350	350	350	350	350	350	350	350	-	-	-	3,150	16,950
Material	95	95	95	95	95	95	95	95	95	-	-	-	855	4,653
Tools & Equipment	140	140	140	140	140	140	140	140	140	-	-	-	1,260	6,450
Other	90	90	90	90	90	90	90	90	90	-	-	-	810	3,748
Total Warranty Costs	10,975	10,975	10,975	10,975	10,975	10,975	10,975	10,975	8,875	-	-	-	96,675	427,581
FAIRFAX PARK														205
Settlements	4	5	6	6	3	6	7	5	5	4	6	4	61	
Warranty Costs														
Service Technician	8,200	8,200	8,200	8,200	8,200	8,200	8,200	8,200	8,200	8,200	8,200	8,200	98,400	329,318
Miscellaneous Labor	2,100	2,100	2,100	2,100	2,100	2,100	2,100	2,100	2,100	2,100	2,100	2,100	25,200	86,400
Truck Expense	350	350	350	350	350	350	350	350	350	350	350	350	4,200	12,600
Material	95	95	95	95	95	95	95	95	95	95	95	95	1,140	4,621
Tools & Equipment	140	140	140	140	140	140	140	140	140	140	140	140	1,680	6,468
Other	90	90	90	90	90	90	90	90	90	90	90	90	1,080	3,968
Total Warranty Costs	10,975	10,975	10,975	10,975	10,975	10,975	10,975	10,975	10,975	10,975	10,975	10,975	131,700	447,275
STONEHENGE														138
Settlements	4	3	4	4	3	4	3	5	3	4	6	4	32	
Warranty Costs														
Service Technician	8,200	8,200	8,200	8,200	8,200	8,200	8,200	8,200	8,200	8,200	8,200	8,200	98,400	342,818
Miscellaneous Labor	2,100	2,100	2,100	2,100	2,100	2,100	2,100	2,100	2,100	2,100	2,100	2,100	25,200	109,920
Truck Expense	350	350	350	350	350	350	350	350	350	350	350	350	4,200	43,920
Material	95	95	95	95	95	95	95	95	95	95	95	95	1,140	6,586
Tools & Equipment	140	140	140	140	140	140	140	140	140	140	140	140	1,680	6,870
Other	90	90	90	90	90	90	90	90	90	90	90	90	1,080	4,018
Total Warranty Costs	10,975	10,975	10,975	10,975	10,975	10,975	10,975	10,975	10,975	10,975	10,975	10,975	131,700	514,132
GRUBBT THICKET														140
Settlements	4	5	6	6	3	6	7						37	
Warranty Costs														
Service Technician	8,200	8,200	8,200	8,200	8,200	8,200	8,200	8,200	8,200	-	-	-	73,800	261,800
Miscellaneous Labor	2,100	2,100	2,100	2,100	2,100	2,100	2,100	2,100	-	-	-	-	16,800	67,500
Truck Expense	350	350	350	350	350	350	350	350	350	-	-	-	3,150	12,025
Material	95	95	95	95	95	95	95	95	95	-	-	-	855	3,355
Tools & Equipment	140	140	140	140	140	140	140	140	140	-	-	-	1,260	4,810
Other	90	90	90	90	90	90	90	90	90	-	-	-	810	2,910
Total Warranty Costs	10,975	10,975	10,975	10,975	10,975	10,975	10,975	10,975	8,875	-	-	-	96,675	352,400

FIGURE 5.1E. Post-Settlement service summary sheet and cost projections.

WARRANTY-SERVICE SUMMARY COST PROJECTIONS
ABC BUILDING COMPANY, INC.
FOR FIVE YEARS BEGINNING JANUARY, 2002

Date: 10/1/02

ACTUAL

Description	Jan-02	Feb-02	Mar-02	Apr-02	May-02	Jun-02	Jul-02	Aug-02	Sep-02	Oct-02	Nov-02	Dec-02	Total
PROJECTIONS													
Settlements	4	4	5	5	4	4	9	9	9	11	11	10	85
ADMINISTRATIVE													
Coordinator	5,175	5,175	5,175	5,175	5,175	5,175	5,175	5,175	5,175	5,400	5,400	5,400	62,775
Administrator	-	-	-	-	-	-	-	-	-	-	-	-	-
Phone Service	80	80	80	80	80	80	80	80	80	95	95	95	1,005
Portfolios	850	-	-	-	-	-	-	-	-	-	-	-	850
Answering Service	-	-	-	95	95	95	95	95	95	100	100	100	870
Office Supplies	216	75	88	283	127	154	205	77	82	150	150	150	1,757
Other	14	23	47	22	61	41	27	14	19	35	35	35	373
Total Admin Costs	6,335	5,353	5,390	5,655	5,538	5,545	5,582	5,441	5,451	5,780	5,780	5,780	67,630
PROJECT COSTS													
Project 1	2,987	2,884	2,863	2,948	2,876	2,872	2,954	2,867	2,872	2,995	2,995	2,995	35,108
Project 2	2,768	2,816	2,828	2,934	2,940	2,932	2,883	2,921	2,899	2,995	2,995	2,995	34,906
Project 3	-	-	-	-	-	-	2,716	3,977	3,897	2,995	2,995	2,995	19,575
Project 4	-	-	-	-	-	-	-	-	3,884	2,995	2,995	2,995	41,612
Project 5													
Total Project Costs	5,755	5,700	5,691	5,882	5,816	5,804	8,553	9,765	13,552	11,980	11,980	11,980	131,201
TOTAL COSTS	12,090	11,053	11,081	11,537	11,354	11,349	14,135	15,206	19,003	17,760	17,760	17,760	198,831
PROJ GROSS INCOME	1,352,000	1,352,000	1,811,500	1,811,500	1,352,000	1,352,000	3,706,500	3,706,500	3,517,500	4,096,500	4,115,500	3,637,000	31,810,500
AS % OF INCOME													0.63%

FIGURE 5.2A. Post-Settlement service summary sheet and cost projections.

Description	Jan-03	Feb-03	Mar-03	Apr-03	May-03	Jun-03	Jul-03	Aug-03	Sep-03	Oct-03	Nov-03	Dec-03	Total
PROJECTIONS													
Settlements	6	7	11	12	8	8	12	14	16	16	13	11	134
ADMINISTRATIVE													
Coordinator	5,650	5,650	5,650	5,650	5,650	5,650	5,650	5,650	5,650	5,650	5,650	5,650	67,800
Administrator	-	-	-	-	-	-	4,000	4,000	4,000	4,000	4,000	4,000	24,000
Phone Service	100	100	100	100	100	100	100	100	100	100	100	100	1,200
Portfolios	1,340												1,340
Answering Service	110	110	110	110	110	110	110	110	110	110	110	110	1,320
Office Supplies	200	200	200	200	200	200	200	200	200	200	200	200	2,400
Other	40	40	40	40	40	40	40	40	40	40	40	40	480
Total Admin Costs	7,440	6,100	6,100	6,100	6,100	6,100	10,100	10,100	10,100	10,100	10,100	10,100	98,540
PROJECT COSTS													
Project 1	4,125	6,025	6,025	6,025	6,025	6,025	6,025	6,025	6,025	6,025	6,025	6,025	70,400
Project 2	4,125	6,025	6,025	6,025	6,025	6,025	6,025	6,025	6,025	6,025	6,025	6,025	70,400
Project 3	4,125	6,025	6,025	6,025	6,025	6,025	6,025	6,025	6,025	6,025	6,025	6,025	70,400
Project 4	4,125	6,025	6,025	6,025	6,025	6,025	6,025	6,025	6,025	6,025	6,025	6,025	70,400
Project 5	-	-	-	-	-	-	-	6,025	6,025	6,025	6,025	6,025	30,125
Total Project Costs	16,500	24,100	24,100	24,100	24,100	24,100	24,100	30,125	30,125	30,125	30,125	30,125	311,725
TOTAL COSTS	23,940	30,200	30,200	30,200	30,200	30,200	34,200	40,225	40,225	40,225	40,225	40,225	410,265
PROJ GROSS INCOME	2,112,000	2,409,500	4,285,500	4,583,000	2,707,000	2,707,000	4,764,000	5,505,000	6,262,000	6,262,000	5,007,500	4,088,500	50,693,000
AS % OF INCOME													0.81%

FIGURE 5.2B. Post-Settlement service summary sheet and cost projections.

Description	Jan-04	Feb-04	Mar-04	Apr-04	May-04	Jun-04	Jul-04	Aug-04	Sep-04	Oct-04	Nov-04	Dec-04	Total
PROJECTIONS													
Settlements	12	13	16	16	7	9	18	20	20	19	19	17	186
ADMINISTRATIVE													
Coordinator	5,900	5,900	5,900	5,900	5,900	5,900	5,900	5,900	5,900	5,900	5,900	5,900	70,800
Administrator	4,200	4,200	4,200	4,200	4,200	4,200	4,200	4,200	4,200	4,200	4,200	4,200	50,400
Phone Service	110	110	110	110	110	110	110	110	110	110	110	110	1,320
Portfolios	1,860												1,860
Answering Service	120	120	120	120	120	120	120	120	120	120	120	120	1,440
Office Supplies	250	250	250	250	250	250	250	250	250	250	250	250	3,000
Other	45	45	45	45	45	45	45	45	45	45	45	45	540
Total Admin Costs	12,485	10,625	10,625	10,625	10,625	10,625	10,625	10,625	10,625	10,625	10,625	10,625	129,360
PROJECT COSTS													
Project 1	8,275	8,275	8,275	8,275	8,275	8,275	8,275	8,275	8,275	8,275	8,275	8,275	99,300
Project 2	8,275	8,275	8,275	8,275	8,275	8,275	8,275	8,275	8,275	8,275	8,275	8,275	99,300
Project 3	8,275	8,275	8,275	8,275	8,275	8,275	8,275	8,275	8,275	8,275	8,275	8,275	99,300
Project 4	8,275	8,275	8,275	8,275	8,275	8,275	8,275	8,275	8,275	8,275	8,275	8,275	108,420
Project 5	8,275	8,275	8,275	8,275	8,275	8,275	8,275	8,275	8,275	8,275	8,275	8,275	99,300
Total Project Costs	41,375	41,375	41,375	41,375	41,375	41,375	41,375	41,375	41,375	41,375	41,375	41,375	505,620
TOTAL COSTS	53,860	52,000	52,000	52,000	52,000	52,000	52,000	52,000	52,000	52,000	52,000	52,000	634,980
PROJ GROSS INCOME	4,305,000	4,675,500	5,984,000	5,984,000	2,498,500	3,077,500	6,922,000	7,582,000	7,582,000	7,211,500	7,211,500	6,551,500	69,585,000
AS % OF INCOME													0.91%

FIGURE 5.2C. Post-Settlement service summary sheet and cost projections.

Description	Jan-05	Feb-05	Mar-05	Apr-05	May-05	Jun-05	Jul-05	Aug-05	Sep-05	Oct-05	Nov-05	Dec-05	Total
PROJECTIONS													
Settlements	21	22	24	27	-	16	26	27	29	30	28	26	276
ADMINISTRATIVE													
Coordinator	6,150	6,150	6,150	6,150	6,150	6,150	6,150	6,150	6,150	6,150	6,150	6,150	73,800
Administrator	4,400	4,400	4,400	4,400	4,400	4,400	4,400	4,400	4,400	4,400	4,400	4,400	52,800
Phone Service	120	120	120	120	120	120	120	120	120	120	120	120	1,440
Portfolios	2,760												2,760
Answering Service	130	130	130	130	130	130	130	130	130	130	130	130	1,560
Office Supplies	300	300	300	300	300	300	300	300	300	300	300	300	3,600
Other	50	50	50	50	50	50	50	50	50	50	50	50	600
Total Admin Costs	13,910	11,150	11,150	11,150	11,150	11,150	11,150	11,150	11,150	11,150	11,150	11,150	136,560
PROJECT COSTS													
Project 1	10,525	10,525	10,525	10,525	10,525	10,525	10,525	10,525	10,525	10,525	10,525	10,525	126,300
Project 2	10,525	10,525	10,525	10,525	10,525	10,525	10,525	10,525	10,525	10,525	10,525	10,525	126,300
Project 3	10,525	10,525	10,525	10,525	10,525	10,525	10,525	10,525	10,525	10,525	10,525	10,525	126,300
Project 4	10,525	10,525	10,525	10,525	10,525	10,525	10,525	10,525	10,525	10,525	10,525	10,525	162,000
Project 5	10,525	10,525	10,525	10,525	10,525	10,525	10,525	10,525	10,525	10,525	10,525	10,525	126,300
Total Project Costs	52,625	52,625	52,625	52,625	52,625	52,625	52,625	52,625	52,625	52,625	52,625	52,625	667,200
TOTAL COSTS	66,535	63,775	63,775	63,775	63,775	63,775	63,775	63,775	63,775	63,775	63,775	63,775	803,760
PROJ GROSS INCOME	7,370,538	7,721,516	8,423,472	9,476,406		5,615,648	9,125,428	9,476,406	10,178,362	10,529,340	9,827,384	9,125,428	96,869,928
AS % OF INCOME													0.83%

FIGURE 5.2D. Post-Settlement service summary sheet and cost projections.

Description	Jan-06	Feb-06	Mar-06	Apr-06	May-06	Jun-06	Jul-06	Aug-06	Sep-06	Oct-06	Nov-06	Dec-06	Total	Grnd Total
PROJECTIONS														
Settlements	21	23	28	26	17	27	29	10	15	13	12	8	229	910
ADMINISTRATIVE														
Coordinator	6,350	6,350	6,350	6,350	6,350	6,350	6,350	6,350	6,350	6,350	6,350	6,350	76,200	351,375
Administrator	4,600	4,600	4,600	4,600	4,600	4,600	4,600	4,600	4,600	4,600	4,600	4,600	55,200	182,400
Phone Service	130	130	130	130	130	130	130	130	130	130	130	130	1,560	6,525
Portfolios	2,290												2,290	9,100
Answering Service	140	140	140	140	140	140	140	140	140	140	140	140	1,680	6,870
Office Supplies	350	350	350	350	350	350	350	350	350	350	350	350	4,200	14,957
Other	55	55	55	55	55	55	55	55	55	55	55	55	660	2,653
Total Admin Costs	13,915	11,625	11,625	11,625	11,625	11,625	11,625	11,625	11,625	11,625	11,625	11,625	141,790	573,880
PROJECT COSTS														
Project 1	10,975	10,975	10,975	10,975	10,975	10,975	10,975	10,975	10,975	10,975	10,975	10,975	131,700	462,808
Project 2	10,975	10,975	10,975	10,975	10,975	10,975	10,975	10,975	8,875	-	-	-	96,675	427,581
Project 3	10,975	10,975	10,975	10,975	10,975	10,975	10,975	10,975	10,975	10,975	10,975	10,975	131,700	447,275
Project 4	10,975	10,975	10,975	10,975	10,975	10,975	10,975	10,975	10,975	10,975	10,975	10,975	131,700	514,132
Project 5	10,975	10,975	10,975	10,975	10,975	10,975	10,975	10,975	8,875	-	-	-	96,675	352,400
Total Project Costs	54,875	54,875	54,875	54,875	54,875	54,875	54,875	54,875	50,675	32,925	32,925	32,925	588,450	2,204,196
TOTAL COSTS	68,790	66,500	66,500	66,500	66,500	66,500	66,500	66,500	62,300	44,550	44,550	44,550	730,240	2,778,076
PROJ GROSS INCOME	7,370,538	8,072,494	9,827,384	9,125,428	5,966,626	9,476,406	10,178,362	3,509,780	5,264,670	4,562,714	4,211,736	2,807,824	80,373,962	329,332,390
AS % OF INCOME													0.91%	0.84%

FIGURE 5.2E. Post-Settlement service summary sheet and cost projections.

THE ABC BUILDING COMPANY, INC.
1234 ANYPLACE DRIVE
ROCKVILLE, MD 20854

Date: _____

PRE-CONSTRUCTION MEETING

Name: _____ Lot # _____ Block/Section_____

Address: _____ Subdivision: _____

Settlement Date: _____

The purpose of the pre-construction meeting is to help develop a relationship between the purchaser and the project manager, to review the contract documents, to review the building program, and to answer questions related to the company and its building program.

Contract Review	Standard Option Review	The Production Process
The Construction Schedule	Interim Inspections	On-Site Safety (no children)

Comments:

_____

_____

_____

_____

_____

Purchasers:

_____   _____
Project Manager

_____   _____
Sales Manager

FIGURE 5.3. Pre-construction meeting form.

THE ABC BUILDING COMPANY, INC.
1234 ANYPLACE DRIVE
ROCKVILLE, MD 20854
Phone: 301/XXX-XXXX Fax: 301/XXX-XXXX

Quality Without Compromise

Date: _____ Lot: _____ Model: _____ Elevation:_____

Inspector:_____   Community:_____

Date on Inventory Control Sheet:_____

Options:_____

QUALITY ASSURANCE PROGRAM

INTL: FRAMING:
____: Check all rough openings and mark jambs
____: Check all windows for size, centerlines, alignment, caulk and tape
____: Check all wall-to-wall kitchen & vanity top conditions
____: Check rough-ins for access panels, scuttles, or pull-down stairs
____: Check rough-ins for all medicine cabinets
____: Check walls for plumb and level
____: Check all blocking and back-up for drywall
____: Check back-up for false beams, handrails, and accessories
____: Check all garage door openings for size and finish detail
____: Check all stud and joist alignment
____: Check all window and door installations; front door 3/4" off the floor
____: Check floor trusses for any unique bearing details and approved connections
____: Check all truss bracing for conformance with designs
____: Check nailing for proper spacing in accordance with schedules
____: Check all jacks, headers, and beams for assembly and quality
____: Check all joist hangers for placement and nailing
____: Check beam pockets, steel beams and columns for proper installation
____: Check all bearing walls for load transfer and proper construction
____: Check spacing and integrity of garage firewalls where required
____: Check all sill sealer
____: Check soffits, bulkheads, and drop ceilings per plans
____: Check all exterior trim for quality of installation
____: Check brick and siding for apparent defects
____: Check back-up for siding
____: Check block-outs for combustion-air venting
____: Check ICS for additional framing options

INTL: PLUMBING
____: Check pressure test on water lines and seal at water service entrance
____: Check all lines for wedges and nail plates
____: Check all rough-in dimensions; tubs, toilet compartments, vanities, kitchen sink, and others
____: Check the location of washer and dryer connections
____: Check all drilling for proper size and location
____: Check for all required fire stopping and insulation of lines in outside walls
____: Check tubs for proper protection and roof flashing for all vent stacks
____: Check clearance and metal angles at top and bottom plates in stack walls
____: Check the integrity and protection of all utility or shower pans
____: Check gas lines and both water and gas meter rack installation
____: Confirm radon venting where required
____: Check ICS for additional plumbing options

FIGURE 5.4. Quality assurance checklist.

Lot:_____ Block:_____

Community:_____

INTL: HEATING, VENTILATION, AND AIR CONDITIONING
____: Check installation of exhaust fans, roof vents, and ventilators
____: Check the thermostat locations and wiring
____: Check installation of range and dryer venting
____: Check locations on all supply and return outlets
____: Check for any conflicts with trim
____: Check for required fire stopping and roof and wall flashing for all vents
____: Check all ductwork for proper fitting and sealing
____: Check installation of dampers
____: Check all framing cut by the HVAC contractor
____: Check all concealed lines
____: Check ICS for additional HVAC options

INTL: ELECTRICAL
____: Check installation of panel, base & outlet
____: Check locations of all outlets and fixtures (incl. TV & phone)
____: Check installation of staples and nail plates
____: Check location and dimensions of recess lighting
____: Check wiring for all bath and attic fans
____: Check wiring for post light
____: Check for conflicts with trim
____: Check kitchen layout and confirm all locations
____: Check ICS for additional electrical options

INTL: INSULATION, AIR STOPPING, AND CORE WALL
____: Check all windows and doors for chinking and taping
____: Check insulation in all recessed entries and overhangs
____: Check for proper caulking at plates, headers, and corners
____: Check installation of house wrap where specified
____: Check all tub decks and plumbing in areas exposed to outside walls
____: Check overhangs, cantilevered decks, bay windows, ceilings and fireplaces
____: Check spacers, caps and the overall integrity of all firewalls

INTL: EXTERIOR
____: Check overall dirt balance on lot
____: Check limits of disturbance and that rough grades conform to the site plan
____: Check for dead or damaged trees and arrange for removal or repairs
____: Check all on-lot and off-lot improvements (retaining wells, drainage inlets, etc.)

NOTED DEFICIENCIES REQUIRING CORRECTION

____:_____
____:_____
____:_____
____:_____
____:_____
____:_____

Completed by:_____

Date:_____

Distribution: white to office following completion; pink field copy to field file

FIGURE 5.4. (continued)

THE ABC BUILDING COMPANY, INC.
1234 ANYPLACE DRIVE
ROCKVILLE, MD 20854

Date: _____

PRE-DRYWALL WALK

Name: _____ Lot # _____ Block/Section_____

Address: _____ Subdivision: _____

Settlement Date: _____

The purpose of the pre-drywall walk is to give the purchaser an opportunity to review the rough structure prior to close-in and to provide a final opportunity to review change orders and options.

Framing & Transfer of Loads	Mechanical System	Plumbing System
Electrical System	Site Conditions & Final Grading	The Orientation

Comments:

_____

_____

_____

_____

_____

Purchasers:

_____   _____

Project Manager

_____

FIGURE 5.5. Pre-drywall walk form.

THE ABC BUILDING COMPANY, INC.
1234 ANYPLACE DRIVE
ROCKVILLE, MD 20852   ORIENTATION CHECKLIST

BUILDING TODAY'S DREAMS AND TOMORROW'S SECURITY

Purchaser:_____ Community:_____ Lot:_____ Date:_____

I/We herby certify that on this date, I/We have participated in a complete orientation of the above listed property, both inside and outside. We have examined finishes including walls, ceilings, glass, mirrors, tile, light fixtures, tubs, showers, vanity tops, sinks, cabinets, counter tops, screens, floors, woodwork, walls, carpeting, and brickwork, and have found them to be free of apparent defects. I/We understand that these items are not warranted after this inspection, at occupancy, or at settlement. Sod, seeding, natural trees, and plantings are also not included under the warranty following settlement.

I/We have been instructed regarding the following equipment, systems, and responsibilities:

☐ HVAC System   ☐ Electrical System   ☐ Plumbing System   ☐ Security (if installed)

☐ Hose Bibs   ☐ Ground-Fault   ☐ Water Valves   ☐ Window Operations

☐ Appliances   ☐ Circuit Breakers   ☐ Paint & Caulking   ☐ Maintenance

I/WE AGREE THAT THE CONSTRUCTION AND COMPLETION OF BOTH THE INSIDE AND OUTSIDE IMPROVEMENTS OF THE HOUSE ARE SATISFACTORY AND ACCEPTABLE, EXCEPT FOR THE ITEMS NOTED BELOW. WE FURTHER AGREE THAT THERE ARE NO OTHER VERBAL OR WRITTEN AGREEMENTS OR COMMITMENTS REGARDING THIS ORIENTATION.

_____   _____   _____
Homeowner Signature   Date   Homeowner Signature

_____   _____
Superintendent Signature   Project Manager Signature

	DATE COMPLETED	HOMEOWNER INITIAL
ITEMS REQUIRING CORRECTION		
1_____		
2_____		
3_____		
4_____		
5_____		
6_____		

FIGURE 5.6. Pre-settlement orientation form.

ORIENTATION CHECKLIST

Purchaser:_____ Community:_____ Lot:_____ Date:_____

ITEMS REQUIRING CORRECTION	DATE COMPLETED	HOMEOWNER INITIAL
7 _____		
8 _____		
9 _____		
10 _____		
11 _____		
12 _____		
13 _____		
14 _____		
15 _____		
16 _____		
17 _____		
18 _____		
19 _____		
20 _____		

All items will be corrected as quickly as possible, but not necessarily before settlement. In the event that items are unable to be completed prior to settlement, Homeowner agrees to provide access as necessary to make such corrections.

_____   _____   _____
Homeowner Completion Signature   Date   Homeowner Completion Signature

_____   _____
Superintendent Signature   Project Manager Signature

Distribution: White to Office Pink to Customer Yellow to Field

FIGURE 5.6. *(continued)*

THE ABC BUILDING COMPANY, INC.
1234 ANYPLACE DRIVE
ROCKVILLE, MD 20854

Date: _____

POST-SETTLEMENT SERVICE REQUEST

Name: _____

Address: _____   Date of Settlement: _____

Community: _____   Lot # _____ Block/Section_____

Work Requested:

☐ _____
☐ _____
☐ _____
☐ _____
☐ _____
☐ _____
☐ _____
☐ _____
☐ _____
☐ _____
☐ _____

The above listed work has been completed with exceptions as noted.

_____   _____
Customer Service Technician   Homeowner

FIGURE 5.7. Post-settlement service request form.

THE ABC BUILDING COMPANY, INC.
1234 ANYPLACE DRIVE
ROCKVILLE, MD 20854

DATE: _____

SETTLEMENT DATE: _____

CUSTOMER SERVICE TECH: _____

SERVICE WORK ORDER

NAME: _____   LOT # _____ BLOCK/SECTION_____

ADDRESS: _____   SUBDIVISION: _____

HOME PHONE: _____   WORK PHONE: _____

SETTTLEMENT DATE: _____

WORK REQUESTED:

_____
_____
_____
_____
_____
_____
_____

WORK PERFORMED: ☐ WARRANTY   ☐ NON-WARRANTY

_____
_____
_____
_____
_____

_____
Customer Service Technician

FIGURE 5.8. Service work order form.

STANDARD POLICIES AND PROCEDURES

THE ABC BUILDING COMPANY, INC.

Date of Implementation: _____

Departmental V.P.: _____

President: _____

FIELD INSPECTION REPORTS

Purpose: The purpose of this policy is to standardize and memorialize field inspection reporting for placement in permanent lot files.

Field Inspection Report

The Field Inspection Report has been designed to standardize our documentation and reporting procedures and to ensure that field reports are submitted to the office for placement in the respective permanent lot file. These reports are meant to supplement, not replace, the Quality Assurance Forms already in use. The report is to be submitted for any noted conditions that are outside the normal parameters of the construction process or in cases where an inspection is conducted at the request of a purchaser or homeowner.

- **Purpose of Inspection:** This block must contain the purpose of the inspection and the reason for its initiation. It is important to note whether the inspection is self-generated or requested by another
- **Notable Conditions:** This includes any conditions that may affect either the ability to accurately conduct an inspection or conditions that are pertinent to the inspection itself. Examples are:
  - Physical conditions of a site that may restrict access or observation
  - The outside temperature at the time of a cooling evaluation
  - Recent rainfall, and amount, prior to a grading inspection
- **Observations:** Be specific and attach photographs if necessary. Do not use generalized language that can be misinterpreted at a later date.
- **Conclusions:** Be specific and direct. Do not make unsupported suppositions. If there is not enough information to draw a conclusion then state that. If a follow up inspection is required then state that. If action is required then state what that action is. If no further action is required then state it as such.

The completed Field Inspection Report is to be submitted to the Inspector's Supervisor for review and submission "up the line". The completed and reviewed report is to be returned to the inspector as a field copy and the original is to be filed in the permanent lot file.

FIGURE 5.9. Field Inspection Report Policy.

a result of a system defect discovered in a neighbor's house. The letter clearly establishes the company's guarantee, the standards for evaluation, and it documents a fair and reasonable effort to deal with the complaint. It sets the stage to close the complaint. In an informal field test that was conducted by the on-site construction manager at the end of last season, temperatures were normal with an outside temperature of 97°; a written report was completed, issued to the homeowner, and placed in the file. Unfortunately, the homeowner has demanded that a technician associated with the third-party contractor who certified the equipment, conduct the test. This arrangement was made by the company at the end of the season and was included it its fee, but hot weather conditions abated before the test could be run.

THE ABC BUILDING COMPANY, INC.
1234 ANYPLACE DRIVE
ROCKVILLE, MD 20854

November 14, 2001

Mr. James H. Lee
5678 Hard Case Dr.
Springfield, VA 22187

Dear Mr. Lee:

I sincerely regret your frustration related to our service schedules. As I explained to you in conversation to-day, we are currently scheduled out two weeks. This backlog has largely resulted for the week that we lost early this month when Bob Tucker was recovering from his surgery. I understand your desire for a timely service response, but I fail to understand the depth of your frustration. Your comments to me were neither warranted nor appreciated. With your statement to "kiss my ass," I think you went well beyond what I consider to be fair and reasonable behavior.

This company has continued to provide timely service since your settlement last July. In early August, you requested out of schedule service on forty-three (43) items, which we completed by the end of the month; in mid-September, you submitted a scheduled list of thirty-two (32) items, which we completed by the end of September; and you are now submitting an out of schedule list of another eighteen (18) items with a demand that we schedule and complete the work by the end of this month. All of these lists have followed, what we consider a routine Orientation and acceptance upon completion, with a list of twenty-seven (27) items that you inspected and signed off prior to your settlement.

As I have indicated to you, this company will continue to provide reasonable post-settlement service in accordance with your warranty and our policies and procedures. You may be assured of our commitment to you and our effort to maintain your goodwill. We have scheduled a service call for you on December 3rd, and we will do everything in our power to complete this work as quickly as possible.

Respectfully,

William C. Smith
President

FIGURE 5.10. Documentation of unacceptable behavior.

The letter to Mr. and Mrs. Brown (Fig. 5.12) represents a very unusual action designed to document the resolution to a problem and to maintain control of a very difficult customer with a valid complaint. It was the decision of the company that this homeowner has reasonable grounds for complaint. The owner travels much of the time, access to the house has been difficult, and the responsible service tech was terminated for his failure to follow-up. The 11-month work is complete in the house, and no additional warranty work is indicated at this time. The homeowner had originally demanded a one-year extension of the entire warranty, including plumbing, mechanical, electrical, and structural. This seemed to be a reasonable compromise.

THE ABC BUILDING COMPANY, INC.
1234 ANYPLACE DRIVE
ROCKVILLE, MD 20854

June 24, 2002

Mrs. Jessica Jones
5678 Routine Case Dr.
Silver Spring, MD 20876

Dear Jessica:

Please be advised that I am in receipt of your email dated June 23, 2002 with respect to your upper level air conditioning system. First, let me restate our position on your air conditioning system for the record. Our warranty with regard to the performance of this system is absolute. As I have indicated in the past, if the system will not perform to the standard for which it was designed, *The ABC Building Company* will accept full responsibility for its repair or replacement. Your system was designed to maintain an average temperature of 75° inside with an outside temperature of 95°. This design standard exceeds the code requirements and most if not all of the standards used in this area, for residential cooling.

Last summer, when we first became aware of your concern for the cooling capacity of your system, this company took the following steps to insure the performance of your system:

- We notified XYZ Mechanical Contractors of your complaint and requested that they evaluate their work and make whatever repairs were required.
- We had another mechanical contractor calculate the loads for your house-type in order to verify that a 2-½ ton system was appropriate for the upper level cooling. Please keep in mind that two of your neighbors with the same house-type have not registered a complaint with their systems. In the case of one of these neighbors, he told me last summer that his system was working just fine.
- We had yet another mechanical contractor conduct a formal evaluation of your system, for which this company paid $250.00 for the inspection, evaluation and certification. Following that inspection, we had XYZ Mechanical Contractors complete some minor, but required work and then received a certification from LMN Mechanical Systems Evaluators that indicated that the <u>equipment</u> was working within the tolerances established by the manufacturer. It was my understanding that you had received a copy of this certification, but I am enclosing it herewith for the record.
- We have also consulted with a representative of the equipment manufacturer. This manufacturer has a good reputation in the industry and we are satisfied that the <u>equipment</u> is appropriate for the loads.

Following this work and certification, I advised you that we would come back and conduct a complete evaluation of inside temperatures and air distribution during a 90°-day, in the event that you were not comfortable. This would have been the next step in proving a system failure. While I recognize that we only had a few 90°-days after this work was completed, I am not aware of any complaint by you during the balance of the summer.

By this letter, be advised that we will extend the warranty on your upper cooling system for another season in order to insure that your system is working in conformance with the design standards. As we have indicated, we are prepared to continue our evaluation as soon as warm weather returns. Please know that we understand your concern and that we will continue to be proactive in this matter. As a result of our voluntary re-inspection of your equipment last month, we have confirmed that a Connor coil has been installed in your second floor system. This coil is fully compatible and, in fact, is sometimes furnished by the equipment manufacturer for installation in their systems. Please understand that the performance of your cooling system is not subjective; it is a matter of science and the standards are clear. I think that if you will reflect on our history and the facts, as you know them, you will conclude that we are acting in good faith and continue to protect your interest.

I will be on vacation the week of March 5th, but I will return to the office the following Monday. I will contact you when I return so that we can further discuss this matter. As always, I appreciate your cooperation and assure you that you can depend on our continued support.

Respectfully,
William C. Smith
President

Encl

FIGURE 5.11. Documentation of an on-going issue.

THE ABC BUILDING COMPANY, INC.
1234 ANYPLACE DRIVE
ROCKVILLE, MD 20854

August 21, 2000

John J. and Jane Brown
5678 Big Mistake Road
Alexandria, VA 33185

Re: Lot 10 B
Fairfax Station

Dear John and Jane:

This letter will confirm our understanding with regard to the warranty on your new home. As a result of this company's failure to provide timely customer service on some list items, I hereby agree to extend your service coverage for an additional year from the date of this letter. This extended coverage will include any reasonable service request, excluding repairs to appliances or other mechanical equipment or devices not specifically covered by the manufacturer or your current Builder's Warranty.

I am enclosing herewith, two Service Request forms for your use. Should you require service, please complete a form and mail or fax it to us. Upon receipt, we will acknowledge it, schedule the work as quickly as possible, and coordinate the service call with you. In the meantime, should you require specific information, or if we can help in any way, please contact our Post-Settlement Service Department.

Again, I appreciate your patience and hope that you will give us the opportunity to regain your confidence. Our primary goal is to maintain your goodwill and you may be assured of our efforts to support a culture of proactive customer care.

Respectfully,

William C. Smith
President

Encl.

FIGURE 5.12. Documentation of resolution to a problem.

THE ABC BUILDING COMPANY, ICN.
1234 ANYPLACE DRIVE
ROCKVILLE, MD 20854

August 3, 2001

Mr. & Mrs. Harvey Green
5678 Apology Court
Germantown, MD 20867

Dear Harvey and Carolyn:

Please accept this letter as a formal apology for my failure to help make your settlement a more pleasant experience. In reflecting on our conversations, and my position related to the toilets and whirlpool tub that were installed in your new home, I realize that I was completely ineffective in my attempts to resolve your complaint. I am certain that had I been more proactive in my approach and more receptive to a compromise position, our relationship may have been preserved and your settlement experience would have been improved.

After reexamining the facts, I have concluded that you were correct. The toilets and the whirlpool tub that were installed by our plumbing contractor do not represent a reasonable substitution; the toilets are an upgrade, with a low profile tank and the tub, while similar, is not the same quality as the one used in the model. Please be advised that I have authorized our plumber make arrangements to convert the toilets to the standard profile and, further, to help you select a suitable substitute for the "model tub", which is now discontinued and not available. In the event that you decide to keep the tub that was provided, we will send you a full refund of the standard option charge, which you paid in the amount of $550.00.

I hope that you will forgive my lack of focus and allow me an opportunity to recover from my mistake. I sincerely hope that you enjoy your new home and that your overall experience with *ABC* has been, and will continue to be, a pleasant one. Please be assured of my personal commitment to you and your family. If I can be of service to you in the future, please contact me on extension #101.

Respectfully,

William C. Smith
President

FIGURE 5.13. Apology letter.

The letter to Mr. and Mrs. Green (Fig. 5.13) is a sincere apology for an error in judgment that was voluntarily reversed without a second request, after discussions with the plumbing contractor. Mr. Smith came to realize that the call came at a time when he was preoccupied with the settlement on a new property. He acted abruptly in dealing with this complaint, which surfaced at the settlement table. When he followed-up after settlement, he realized his mistake.

It is interesting to note that Mr. Smith has chosen to open his routing letters by using first names and harsh letters with the formal prefix. He also ends each letter with respectfully, which indicates reasonable consideration for every customer.

DOCUMENT CUSTOMER SATISFACTION

Customer satisfaction is the primary goal of a proactive customer care program. Customer satisfaction is not only a requirement that insures the highest level of performance, it is also a requirement for referral sales. In order to measure the company's success in the area of customer satisfaction, it must conduct satisfaction surveys. The obligation to evaluate performance is ongoing, as is the need for constant improvement. It is only through this process that companies can achieve benchmark status. It validates the effectiveness of the customer care process that has been implemented, it identifies areas that require improvement, and it can help the company measure other consumer attitudes that are critical to the success of a building operation.

The company should also encourage its customers to record their satisfaction with letters that the company can retain. Testimonials should be solicited softly and cherished when they arrive. Such letters are an indication of performance, although they must not be used to measure success; that can only be accomplished through formal and informal surveys. Testimonials can, however, serve as evidence that the company cares, and has a good track record for customer satisfaction. They also memorialize the attitudes of a number of homeowners who could be used for references or to document the company's effort to maintain the goodwill of its customers.

In some cases, home builders will contract with third parties to conduct focus groups of current homeowners in order to measure attitudes related to a number of topics including customer service. Professional moderators and the required facilities can be expensive, but it can be an activity well worth the cost. A dose of reality can go a long way toward improvement. Production builders with a volume of more than two hundred units per year should probably have focus groups conducted annually in order to measure attitudes on a number of topics.

SATISFACTION SURVEYS

The requirement to conduct satisfaction surveys is absolute for those with a proactive customer care program. They are necessary to validate the success of the process, to provide direction for improvement, and to demonstrate the depth of the commitment to customer care. Such surveys can be either informal survey conducted by the company, or they may be formal surveys conducted by a third-party contractor. Most small custom and low-volume home builders will depend on informal surveys conducted by the company in order to avoid the considerable expense associated with third-party contractors. In truth, I believe informal surveys should be a standard practice for all home builders. This type of activity will help maintain the proper focus in larger companies and help the front-line staff monitor the pulse on a day-to-day basis. They will also produce additional information that can be compared against the contracted survey results.

Informal Surveys

Informal surveys might include a bi-fold survey form designed to measure attitudes at the time of settlement. Such surveys could be given to purchasers by the title officer at the end of the settlement for inclusion in the settlement package. A series of short questions could be designed to measure customer satisfaction in a number of areas, but should specifically include the performance of both the sales manager and the construction manager for the project; this would establish accountability for these key employees. Although the response may be a slightly distorted by the normal frustrations that occur with closings, the participation would be close to one hundred percent.

Following settlement, it may be appropriate to conduct a post-settlement survey immediately following the sixty-day service call. Again, a short list of questions could be designed to measure attitudes about the product and warranty service, as well as the performance of the service technician. The form could be a card and the technician could turn it in with the completed list; again, producing almost one hundred percent participation and a valuable document for the file.

In addition to these two informal surveys, follow-up phone calling can be a good tool to insure customer satisfaction. Random calls, or calls to targeted customers with a written record can help employees and staff check and memorialize the attitudes of its customers. In all cases, such calls should produce a document for the file. Such calls can be part of a routine follow-up procedure or used to check performance and demonstrate a proactive response following a special event or activity with a customer. Although informal surveys lack the science and detachment of third-party surveys, they can be useful, particularly for the smaller company that may lack the financial resources required for professional surveys.

Third-Party Satisfaction Survey

Surveys prepared and conducted by a professional third-party are likely to provide the best information for improvement. There is a science to survey preparation and techniques, and these are the people familiar with it. These survey results provide high quality facts upon which management can apply solutions that will improve customer satisfaction. Benchmark companies rely on facts and this technique is one of the best sources of information on the overall operation of a business that maintains a customer focus.

In most cases, home builders try to survey their homeowners at 60 days following the closing and again at the end of the first year. Surveys are reported quarterly, with tabulations for the past quarter, as well as the last 12-month period. Historically, response rates fall between seventeen and twenty percent of the total population with a slightly higher negative results.

THE LINEAR EXCEPTION

Customer care is a circular process; that is, it is never ending. When a customer calls, the company will provide assistance in some form. Although the company would not be willing to commit to sending a technician with tools three years after settlement, it would send a technician or construction manager to inspect a condition that may very well be covered, or, perhaps, to offer advice that will help a homeowner with a maintenance issue. This is not the case, however, with our toughest customers; they are the linear exception. We must move away from them to reduce the friction in our operations. If the company delivers 600 units per year, they must manage approximately 12 tough customers on a rotating basis (2% of the total); if a national or regional company delivers

30,000 units per year, they must manage approximately 600 of these toughest customers on a rotating basis. The only way it can work is if the company moves away from them after the company has clearly met its obligations.

Dealing with this group is a challenge and if you have 600 of them each year, you have an enormous potential for trouble; approach them with caution, not fear. Yard signs, picketing, bad press, and litigation are all possibilities. This is the group that will apply their resources to discredit responsible builders and their staff. They will try to unite other homeowners into class action litigation (particularly the 8% who have become quiet), they will try to influence the attitudes of homeowner associations, and they can be the poison that contaminates a new community for a builder or senior manager who loses focus. In short, they have the capacity to create very serious damage to a builder's reputation. Just about every national and regional homebuilder has had some unhappy experience with this group, and many have sustained considerable damage as a result of their lack of preparedness. It appears that very few employees are able to confront the insatiable appetite of the national media and articulate the conditions that produce such an anomaly. Companies with long-standing reputations for ethical behavior and proactive customer should simply not be subjected to such poor treatment. For those who have failed to meet their responsibilities, it is time to join the 21st century; without proactive customer care you will not survive.

It is my hope that this book will create a greater awareness on the part of those who work with these people every day, as well as those who listen to them without knowing who they really are. The only way that we can effectively deal with this group is through public awareness. It is a very sensitive subject, but we can all educate the public slowly. In the future, when responsible builders become tangled in a public exposure with these customers, perhaps this book will help. For those insensitive employees who would rush to judgment and deny any customer reasonable care and attention, beware; responsible builders will simply have to replace you with someone who is prepared to reserve judgment, maintain a professional attitude, and manage the toughest customer.

PART IV SERVICE ISSUES OR DISPUTES

Complaints begin when customers arrive. Comments in this section focus on those complaints that are received by customers and relate to the building process. Customer complaints are typical, and occur before, during, or after construction. Other complaints include those a home builder might receive from neighbors, community associations, municipal inspectors, lenders, investors, or others, who have been ignored.

Solutions depend on the answer to one very basic question:
what is fair and reasonable?

CHAPTER 6

COMMON SERVICE ISSUES OR DISPUTES

PRE-CONSTRUCTION

Most of the complaints that are received from customers before construction starts are initiated during the purchase process; they are related to the sales, contracting, or the selection process. They include the following:

CONTRACTING AND SALES PROCESSING

Complaints that result from poorly written contracts and poorly coordinated marketing materials are some of the most difficult to handle because the documents speak for themselves. What would a reasonable person assume? This can be very damaging if the company has failed to provide the necessary care and attention to these critical documents in the first place.

Contract Omissions
In preparation for contracting, all contract documents should be carefully reviewed by staff for consistency and statements of fact, and by an attorney for legal content. It is only with such detailed effort that disputes related to or resulting from these documents can be avoided. After the purchaser has executed a sales contract, it must be reviewed very carefully for content before an officer of the company ratifies it. A very responsible senior manager should complete this review and the contract should then be modified if necessary and ratified. In such an event, keep in mind that the contract is now incomplete and unenforceable until such time as the purchaser acknowledges the modifications. Loosely written contracts that require modification after the purchaser signs, can provide an opportunity for the purchaser to withdraw the contract if they should decide to do so.

Poorly Coordinated Collateral Sales Materials
Sales specifications, plans, feature sheets, option descriptions, and displays are all critical sales tools that help purchasers understand what they have purchased. In many cases, inaccuracies in these materials can cause considerable misunderstandings and misconceptions at the time of the sale. Unless these materials are well coordinated, they can become the focus of controversy after ratification of the contract. In some cases, such controversy

may not develop until a feature has been executed in the field during construction; condition that can have considerable consequences for both the buyer and the builder.

Advertising Inaccuracies

Although advertising inaccuracies do not occur often, they do occur and can become a point of controversy. In most cases, the question will be, has the company misrepresented a material fact? If the answer is yes, it may have committed a fraud. All advertising should be carefully reviewed when insertion orders are initiated. A failure to take the time necessary to insure accuracy can create a very large expense or the loss of goodwill later on.

Non-Standard Options

Unfortunately, non-standard option procedures can be a very large point of frustration for homebuyers. Most sales managers are poorly prepared to describe the non-standard option in a legal form that will avoid confusion, and builders often take forever to price and process such requests. In many cases, the reality of the final pricing produces additional disappointment, when the sales manager has not properly prepared purchasers. For most builders, the non-standard option is a necessary evil that they would like to avoid. Unfortunately, it is a reality of our competitive industry and a process that creates accurate descriptions and timely pricing must be developed in order to minimize frustration and the potential for disputes.

SOLUTION

When dealing with such complaints, apply the reasonable person standard and make a judgment about the intent of the documents. Are the documents clear, or is it more likely that a reasonable person would interpret the documents the same way as the purchaser? If this can only be answered in favor of the purchaser, then the only action is to either perform in accordance with the documents, as you perceive them, or to appeal to the purchaser to permit you to write a clarification addendum that will remove the confusion and any unintentional obligation. Even in the event that it seems clear to you, you should offer to prepare an addendum for clarification. Failing that, you should have a senior staff member review the issue and make a determination. Again, the reasonable person standard will still be the test.

THE SELECTION PROCESS

Complaints related to the selection process often center around a failure to disclose all of the options or materials that are available, disputes over what was meant by the option description, or pricing standards.

Standard Option Selections

Unless standard options are well organized, described properly, priced fairly, and offered to every purchaser, the results create considerable frustration and disappointment for homebuyers. Nothing will disappoint a purchaser more than to find out from a neighbor, after settlement, that an option that they thought was not available or that they were not aware of, was, in fact, executed for others.

Material Selections

The potential for frustration, confusion, and mistakes increase considerably unless the selection process is controlled by the builder. When builders send their purchasers to a vendor's showroom, they surrender control of the process and set themselves up for unhappy customers. Unreasonable upgrades, unexpected material delays, price gouging, production conflicts, and unhappy customers are often the result of such a mistake. By maintaining a well-organized display center in a model home, or a centralized design center, dedicated to providing only current material samples and a wide range of controlled upgrades and pricing, the builder maintains control of both the sale and the impact of such selections on the construction process.

Pricing

Complaints related to pricing objections are not difficult to handle. Pricing standards should reflect reasonable strategies; margins on some options should be lower than they are on others, either because they are more difficult to execute, or prices are more easily compared. All option pricing should be established based on a survey of competitors in a specific market area. Sales managers must be prepared to deal with this objection by informing the customer. By restating the pricing policies and inviting the customer to compare.

SOLUTION

The only way to be successful here is to be well organized and keep sales managers informed. These types of complaints are driven by frustration and disappointment after the fact, when there is little you can do to make amends. The question here is what is fair and reasonable; in most cases all you can do is inform the customer and apologize. In the event that a customer can establish a strong argument as it relates to option descriptions, all you can do is negotiate your way out; keep in mind that others with the same option will follow with the same complaint.

DURING CONSTRUCTION

Complaints that are typically received during the construction process stem from a very broad category of issues related to the construction start, change orders, access issues, the construction process, construction scheduling, construction quality, fit and finish issues, or the level of communication between the company and the customer.

CONSTRUCTION START

Complaints related to the construction start center around a failure to start construction when it was predicted.

Re-sites

A re-site occurs when a purchaser buys a house other than the one that has already been sited on the lot. In such cases, the engineer must redraw the plan reflecting the new house type; often, this means a new first floor elevation and adjustments to the grading. In those cases where the engineer is backed-up, it means delays and the permit cannot usually be submitted without the site plan.

Permit Processing

The permit process has become very complicated today. Most jurisdictions publish very clear guidelines for the application process and the local building departments then try to complete reviews quickly and issue permits, but not all. Many times, the review process becomes backed-up, permits are delayed, and sometimes for unreasonable periods of time.

Weather Condition

Starts can become difficult when weather conditions don't cooperate. Cold and wet weather are the big culprits. In come cases, these delays can become considerable; fortunately, this is not usually the case and even when a start is delayed due to weather, an experienced construction manager can usually make up all or part of the lost time.

SOLUTION

Try to set reasonable expectations during the sales process. To accomplish this, sales managers must be informed about lead-time for permit processing. Or, they must at least prepare the customer for the possibility of delay.

CHANGE ORDER PROCESSING

Change orders are a necessary evil for most builders. They are required to satisfy the needs of the customer and to improve the bottom line, but they also have the effect of delaying construction, confusing the buyer, and creating disputes. Often, complaints after construction starts center around the ability of the company to accept a change order and execute it, without unnecessarily delaying the process and increasing the builder's cost.

Processing Delays

Often, builders would rather avoid such changes, but have a problem saying no. As a result, those who are required to price and process such change orders can be poorly focused, which can cause delays that only compound the problem.

Confusion

Such change orders often cause confusion because they are generally discussed with construction managers before any paperwork is initiated. In the worse cases, some project managers will execute the change order before it has been approved and paid for in order to keep production on schedule. In other cases well-meaning construction managers will approve a change without understanding that it may take a week or two just to get the purchaser to sign off on the paperwork . . . more delays and additional hidden costs.

Material Availability
When specialty materials are not checked before the execution of a change order, the construction manager may be surprised at the back-order time required when he goes to execute the change.

SOLUTION

Have a very clear process for expediting such change orders; establish a policy and say "no" if you must; it will minimize hard feelings in the long run and help the buyer understand the need for timely execution.

ACCESS ISSUES

Most buyers feel they have the right to see the house whenever they want, under any conditions.

Policy
In most cases, buyers are just that; they have rights as a purchaser, but not ownership rights. Company policy should be clear about access to the construction site; it should establish a time for such inspections, under controlled conditions that consider the safety of the contract purchaser or owner, and it should require a representative of the company (either a sales manager, a construction manager, or a responsible assistant). Sales and construction managers must understand that they are, under no conditions, to give a key to a purchaser and give them permission to enter a house without a representative of the company. Policy and scopes of work should also make it clear to tradesmen that they are not to take instructions from an owner.

Third-Party Inspectors
Third-party inspectors should not be encouraged, but it is a buyer's right to obtain such support if they feel that it is necessary. Such inspectors should be made to feel comfortable and treated with respect. In the unlikely event that such an inspector displays a level of disrespect, is unfair in his or her statements, or otherwise threatens the relationship of the builder with his customer, he or she should not be allowed to conduct future inspections; keep in mind that if a builder excludes such an inspector, the company had better be ready to defend the position in court based on clear facts.

In thirty-five years, I know of only one such inspector and his results are well documented in the counties where building departments have had to defend their own actions to buyers who have become very concerned as a result of unfair inspection reports. In this case, it was simply easier to defend the position in a court of law than it was to allow the inspector to destroy relationships that the company had taken such care to establish. The exclusion of this inspector was established by a well-drafted letter, directed to the specific inspector, and delivered by certified mail . . . end of problem.

Delivery of Keys at Settlement

Believe it or not, even keys can become a problem for homebuilders. In most cases, builders rely on master keys during the construction process and it is not until settlement that the actual keys for the house are presented to the homeowner. All too often, the keys do not arrive at the settlement office in time, or they are not well protected and presented in a professional manner. Keys are security devices and homeowners become very concerned if they are not treated with care.

SOLUTION

Cover as much as possible in the contract of sale, policy statements, and scopes of work. Require the sales manager to inform the buyer, repeat the policy discussion at the pre-construction meeting, and hope for a reasonable result. Everyone must understand that control is the key requirement here. Never let anyone challenge the quality of your process unfairly; it could have a very negative effect if it became part of a discovery document in a legal dispute down the road.

CONSTRUCTION PROCESS

These complaints include a variety of issues and concerns advanced by customers during construction. In most cases, they relate to how we do thing, the quality of labor, the application of materials, and reasonable care and oversight. In some cases, these complaints are well founded, even in a company with a proactive customer care program.

Ignorance and Misunderstanding

There is a great deal of ignorance and misunderstanding concerning about the new home construction process that we employ in the United States in the 21st Century. Most expect a process more akin to the auto industry with well engineered processes and sub-processes that go together smoothly under controlled conditions. Instead, they see a process that may or may not be well defined; a process using a combination of skilled, semi-skilled, and poorly trained labor. A process that is subject to weather conditions, labor shortages, material shortages, and sometimes, an unacceptable level of ignorance. Our process has the ability to confuse and frustrate our buyers; and very few of us have the ability to articulate such inherent obstacles to the satisfaction of those who simply do not understand.

Discontinued Material Selections

Most customers are disappointed when they find out that a material that they have selected has been discontinues. Styles are discontinued and colors change, both of which have the potential to create considerable disappointment.

SOLUTION

Try to help buyers understand the process up front, rather than appearing defensive when something goes wrong. Use sales managers to explain the process, prepare the customer for the possibility of discontinued material, and to maintain a line of communication during the construction process. Require construction managers to discuss the process in detail during pre-construction meetings and give the customer the opportunity to approve substitutions when materials are discontinued or otherwise not available.

CONSTRUCTION SCHEDULING

Most complaints related to construction scheduling result from the buyer's need or desire to move as quickly as possible, or simply the builder's failure to keep the buyer informed. Lost time is not accepted easily by a purchaser who has sold his or her house and is under contract with a firm settlement date; some are living in temporary conditions that are almost never satisfactory; and, still others may be commuting long distances on weekends until the house is finished and they can move their families.

Scheduling Methods

The method of construction scheduling is less important than the fact that schedules are maintained and monitored. Some of the most fundamental systems can work well if the staff understands them and is dedicated to reasonable cycle-time for the product they are building. Construction managers and trade contractors must be held accountable, and others in the company must have a reporting system so that they can help the customer by providing periodic updates.

Delays

In most cases, unexpected delays are frustrating to both staff and customers. In most cases, staff will discusses the impact of delays during construction and the need to make up time, but no one bothers to discuss conditions with the customer. In a proactive company, sales managers will make it a point to stay informed and to pass critical information on to the customer when delays occur. Some builders today are providing such tracking information to buyers through the Internet.

SOLUTION

The solution is to establish responsibilities, maintain a system, require weekly reporting, reward performance, and keep the customer informed. Unless the customer understands the reporting process and the sales manager provides information on a regular basis, purchasers will generally drive a good construction manager crazy. Be proactive and protect everyone's interest by developing a system that works.

CONSTRUCTION QUALITY

This includes a variety of complaints regarding the labor, the material applications, and the management of the construction process.

Oversight Issues

Most customers are very aware of management's failure to provide reasonable oversight. Too often they see trades working without adequate supervision, they witness mistakes that are repeated over and over, and they see a very slow moving process that goes without activity for long periods. This can only produce frustration and a loss of confidence in the builder.

Defects in Labor and Material

Unfortunately, on occasion, our most intense customers will identify defects in labor and material before we do. They may respond with unreasonable frustration and assume that no one is watching the store. Or, in other cases, the construction manager may be aware of a condition that he or she intends to correct during a punch-out period. When customers bring us complaints regarding labor and material, we must take them seriously. Both the complaint and the resolution should be documented for the file.

Failure to Properly Execute Options

This condition can result from either a poorly organized construction program or a new trade contractor who is not familiar with the option descriptions and requirements. Both standard and non-standard options can be affected and customers almost always attribute such failures to a lack of organization.

Lack of Reasonable Care in the Finishing Process

Customers will never be sympathetic when they see dirt tracked into their new homes by tradesmen working on the finishing process or drywall dust in their carpeting, as a result of careless sanding during punch-out. General housekeeping during the finishing process is a good measure of the quality of management; after all, what would you want in your own house?

SOLUTION

In those cases in which a quality building program is obvious to the buyer, they will instinctively maintain a higher level of trust and comfort with the process. The best way to deal with these objections is to avoid them. Be sure that your construction managers are well qualified; that they involve the customer; that they provide a higher level of oversight; that they perform frame checks and floor checks; that they complete a quality assurance check list; and, that *the company compensates them fairly for such extraordinary effort,* uses uniform contract documents, and maintains an effective partnership program with its trade contractors and suppliers.

FIT AND FINISH ISSUES

Fit and finish complaints are common and some of the most difficult to deal with. If the construction manager and the trade contractors that he or she supervises lack the discipline to produce finishes that will meet the expectations of the buyers or that are representative of local building standards, this battle is lost before it begins. High standards of fit and finish must be maintained by the company in order to minimize such complaints; although the quality of fit and finish can be a subjective question, the test will be reasonable expectations and local building standards. For this reason, I favor using the same standards of fit and finish in model homes as those that will be characteristic of the production process. In cases where the model demonstrates a higher level of fit and finish, the model will become the standard advanced by the buyers, and they will be absolutely right.

Interior Trim, Drywall, and Paint

A failure to maintain reasonable standards her will be costly. In too many cases, production houses are delayed following the orientation in order that trade contractors refinish the house in order to meet a reasonable standard; the builder's biggest nightmare begins when a home that has failed to meet reasonable standards of fit and finish is acknowledged after occupancy and the homeowner then has to endure finishing trades repairing trim, patching and sanding drywall, painting, cleaning, and otherwise punching out, what should have been a finished home. This action can create considerable risk to the builder and almost always results in the loss of goodwill. Such a condition can only be the result of a failure in the production process.

Finish-in-place Hardwood Floors

Finished-in-place hardwood floors can be another nightmare if they are not protected during the finishing process, or in the event that the finish does not perform as it should. After delivery, furniture must be moved, floors must be sanded or at least screened, both of which create a fine dust, they must be finish coated, and they must be allowed to dry. All at great hardship and inconvenience for the homeowner. When it comes to finished-in-place hardwood floors, as it is with all fit and finish, it is critical that the builder get it right the first time.

SOLUTION

Management must understand what standard is a fair and reasonable standard, maintain a proper sequence of construction, provide necessary heat, light, and power, and hold the trade contractors accountable or replace them when necessary.

POOR COMMUNICATION

This is probably the biggest complaint about the construction process. Once the construction begins, sales managers have a tendency to let a sleeping dog lie, construction managers are too busy with the day-to-day, and the customer has no idea what to do. In most cases, they only get information as a result of their own effort.

Everyone in the Company Should Monitor Production Reports

If everyone has the ability to provide information, it will make things easier for everyone. This should not excuse those who are responsible for keeping the customer informed, but it will help others in the company support the effort. In the event that internal production schedules are discussed with customers, they must be continuously reminded that the schedules are intended for management use and the buyer must rely on the written notices that they will receive from the company in preparation for a closing.

Setting Expectations

Expectations should be set early with homebuyers. Sales managers have an ongoing opportunity to set expectations and construction managers can make it a part of the Pre-Construction Meeting and Pre-Drywall Walk. Everyone in the company should learn the skill of setting expectations . . . under-promise and over-deliver.

Use Sales Managers as the Shepherds

Sales managers should be used as the shepherds for buyers following settlement; after settlement, it becomes the job of the customer care coordinator. Each must understand that communication is critical, but it must be controlled.

Effects of Production Delays

In most cases, the customer will accept routine delays that occur during the construction process with some disappointment. Most of the time, such delays will impact them in negative ways, but they will accept it and move on. Nothing, however, will set a buyer off like a last minute delay that causes them to reschedule plans related to a move and settlement. It has been my experience that proactive companies will have a "late house policy" to cover such situations. A policy that requires the most senior construction manager to take charge when it becomes necessary to reschedule a closing date; to contact the purchaser and to coordinate the re-scheduled Orientation and delivery in a very personal way.

Making Numbers at Year-End

Forcing the delivery of a house in order to improve year-end numbers can be a very risky and costly undertaking. Sometimes referred to, as "slamming houses" or "crunching schedules" at year-end, it is not an unusual exercise in large public companies. In cases where such decisions do not include the buyer, the customer may object and feel short changed at the end of the day. It has been my experience that with a little controlled effort, the excitement of the new house can be preserved for the customer and the builder can still capture the closing for year-end. Try this procedure the next time you want to push a house for year-end:

1. A senior construction manager should contact the purchaser at least 30-days prior to year-end. Explain that the company thinks that it can complete the house for year-end, but it may be close, offer an incentive to your buyer (extra landscaping, a deck extension, or perhaps a molding package that was not taken), and then ask the customer if they would like you to push for completion by year-end. If they agree, explain that the risk is that the house may be a little rough and require additional work the first week of January, in which case, you would, conduct an inspection with them, give them a letter of assurance, and postpone the actual orientation until the house is fully complete the first or second week in January. This will work particularly well where the buyer wants the tax credits and is under no

pressure to move. Assure the buyer that you will stay with them, give reports as work progresses, and be there at completion of the house.

2. Follow-up with a letter that outlines the agreement and describes the consideration (the landscaping, deck extension, or molding package) and restate exactly what the process will be.
3. Make a call to the buyer two weeks out and again at one week out.
4. If the house in fact makes it, complete an orientation and thank the customer personally for his or her cooperation. If the house does not make, conduct an inspection of the house with the purchaser and provide them with a very carefully crafted letter that outlines the missing work and provides a date certain for the orientation after settlement. Never lose site of the fact that this procedure is based on trust; *it must not be violated or the consequences could be severe.*

I used this process one year to close five homes representing more than $3 million dollars in gross income; each homeowner was satisfied with the program and in two of the five cases, the buyers thanked me profusely. In most cases, the post-settlement punch-out will continue beyond what is reasonable, but that is the price you pay for working outside the normal process and it was more than justified given the importance of booking the income that year. Sometimes, it is simply a matter of how it is presented to the customer and the care and attention that you are willing to extend. For those builders working on a fiscal year rather than a calendar year, it would probably be slightly more difficult to get the cooperation of the buyer. In these cases, the builder must be very careful *not to force the customer into a position that is unfair and unreasonable* simply to improve the financial performance of the company.

SOLUTION

Never avoid the customer regardless of your position. Remember who you work for and understand that communication is a key to protecting yourself from your most difficult customers and helping the others develop a much higher opinion of you and your company. Learn to manage your effort by communicating more effectively and remember that an emotional response does nothing to improve the process. "Customer care is not a department, it is a state of mind."

AFTER DELIVERY

Most home builders today use an industry-standard, ten-year limited express warranty. Under most national ten-year warranty programs, the home builder warrants the home to be free of faulty workmanship or materials and major structural defects for the first year; that the structure, HVAC, electrical, and plumbing systems will be free of defects for the second year; and then an insurance underwriter maintains a major structural warranty from years three through ten. Such warranty programs are costly and generally only accept builders based on experience, proof of financial responsibility, and references, but they provide a higher level of assurance for new homebuyers.

In all cases, construction managers, service managers, service coordinators, and service technicians must review such written documents and become familiar with the obligations, conditions, and procedures established by the documents. In all cases, some standards of evaluation or statements of responsibility are published in the warranty document, and everyone involved in the post-settlement warranty service process must be aware of them. Although they should only be used in unique situations, a copy of these standard form documents should be available to service technicians for use with homeowners who are not well informed about the responsibilities of builders and owners; often, the confusion between warranty service and normal homeowner maintenance is addressed in such documents, and these documents are often provided to buyers at the time of contract and again, when they are executed at closings.

Post-settlement warranty service includes everything that occurs after the closing of the property. In a company with a proactive customer care program, the requirements should be relatively easy. They should not include repetitive service problems that have been removed as a result of the Quality Building Process. Some such problems include the following:

◆ Water leaks created by poor window installation, flashing problems, defective plumbing joints, or poor grading

◆ Floor squeaks that exceed what is normal

◆ Mortar joints that are loose and cracking from winter frost

◆ Walls and floors that are out of plumb and level

◆ Line cracking in ceramic tile

◆ Scratched glazing resulting from careless masons

◆ Unreasonable irregularities in walls from bowed studs

◆ Ductwork that has not been connected

◆ Poorly anchored rails and bath accessories

◆ Poor drywall finishes resulting from unacceptable installation and finishing practices

◆ Rough paint finishes resulting from the lack of care in preparation

◆ Missing ceiling insulation

◆ Inconsistent door swings

◆ Unacceptable carpet seams

◆ Screens and other common parts on backorder

Recognize any of these conditions? They are fairly common complaints in many home building companies. In fact, without a quality building program, many of these complaints will become repetitive and almost predictable.

STRUCTURAL ISSUES

Any complaint related to a potential structural issue must be treated as an emergency. They are the most damaging complaints against home builders and they are the most difficult to defend.

Investigate them quickly using the most qualified employees, seek second opinions, use third-party inspectors if necessary, and document both the evaluation process (field inspection reports) and solutions (engineering reports). Structural issues can be the most damaging for a home builder and must be attacked with a strong sense of urgency.

SOLUTION

Builders must be proactive in this area and resolve issues quickly will little regard for ultimate liability. Evaluate conditions quickly, take pictures, involve third-party inspectors, obtain legal advice, but move quickly and get involved at the very highest level. Such complaints should raise a red flag for every employee. If a structural issue develops with one of your most difficult customers, you may need strategies and initiatives that only an owner or company president can manage.

WATER LEAKS

Complaints related to water leaks usually bring with them, serious concern for interior finishes such as carpet and pad, drywall, insulation, and the like. Nothing will frustrate a new homeowner more, because so many have bad experiences with leaks in the past, or have heard the horror stories.

Next to structural complaints, water problems are the most serious service issues for homeowners and often present puzzling conditions that delay resolution. The contents of a structure are often damaged or placed at risk as a result of a leak or prolonged exposure to moisture, some property damage is almost assured (both damage to the finishes of the structure and possibly to the contents), mold and mildew is a sensitive issue today, and homeowners have a tendency to become frustrated and unsympathetic when initial efforts fail to control the problem. Because of the critical nature of water problems, construction managers often become involved in evaluating conditions and directing the efforts to overcome such problems.

There are five primary areas which subject a structure to potential water problems: (1) plumbing pipes and fixtures, (2) the roof, (3) wall assemblies, and (4) the foundation, and (5) storm water management.

Plumbing Leaks—These leaks typically occur in shower pans or the supply and waste lines of the plumbing system and are generally more easily diagnosed and corrected. A leak in a supply line is typically continuous because the water is under pressure, while leaks in waste lines and shower pans are intermittent because they only leak when they are used. Some typical leaks include the following:

Leaks Related to Waste Lines

◆ *Clogged drains*—may occur as a result of construction or other debris collecting in traps or areaway drains; such leaks are easily identified and corrected. On the other hand, a clogged condensate drain in the pan under the condensing coil of an air conditioner will produce an almost continuous leak during warm weather when the air conditioner is functioning continuously; this is particularly troublesome where the air handler is located in the attic and a back-up drain is also non-functional.

◆ *Defective joints*—unlike the joints in supply lines that are under pressure, joints occurring in waste lines seldom leak. Where such leaks occur, they are generally around traps. Such leaks can be avoided by requiring the plumber to plug all openings and fill waste lines with water before concealment.

◆ *Shower pan leaks*—are leaks in a built-up shower pan resulting from the inadequate construction of the pan, damage to the pan (such as that created by a drywall nail that has been stepped on after the pan is installed), or a defective seal at corners or the drain. Such problems can usually be verified by taping the drain with duct tape, filling the pan with two inches of water, and waiting for the leak to occur. Such leaks are expensive to cure because, in most cases, the shower base must be removed and reconstructed; these leaks can be avoided by using a prefabricated, molded shower receptor, or by filling the pan with water after installation and before drywall and leaving it until the ceramic tile contractor installs the tile.

◆ *Defective seals at fixtures*—wax rings installed at toilet flanges will sometimes leak after the fixture has been used for some time. In most cases, the installation is defective and the ring must be replaced. Some builders will use a gasket rather than a wax ring to help avoid such problems.

Leaks Related to Supply Lines

◆ *Defective joints*—unlike waste lines, supply lines are under constant pressure of 35 psi (pounds per square inch) or more, and therefore are more likely to experience joint failure. When a supply line joint fails, the flow is continuous (until the main water valve is closed in most cases) and property damage, inconvenience, and frustration are generally present. Such leaks are generally not difficult to find and, almost always, require the removal of some wall or ceiling finish material, which then must be repaired after the defective joint has been corrected. Such leaks can be largely avoided by requiring the plumbing contractor to pressure test all supply lines before concealment;

ends are capped, a temporary pressure gauge is installed, and compressed air is inserted and monitored for a twenty-four hour period.

◆ *Frost damage*—can occur as a result of a pipe freezing; in cases where winter conditions are severe, or where a pipe is improperly protected, it may freeze and then cause a continuous leak as it thaws out. Such leaks can be avoided by keeping supply lines in interior walls and floors over heated spaces. Where supply lines must be located in exterior walls or floors (including walls and floors adjacent to unheated garages) increased wall thickness, additional insulation (including pipe wraps), and ambient heat may be provided to prevent such freezing.

◆ *Puncture damage*—occurs when a fastening device such as a nail is inadvertently driven into a supply line during the trim stage. Such conditions often occur where the plumber has not properly protected his line where it passes through top plates where crown molding is to be installed; in copper piping it is not uncommon for the nail to seal itself and then to appear months later as the nail rusts. Such conditions can be avoided by requiring the plumbing contractor to install "kick" plates and then inspecting them prior to concealment, when a formal inspection of the structure is made.

Roof Leaks—are leaks that relate to the roof and typically result from construction defects or extraordinary weather conditions in a region where such conditions are not anticipated by building code requirements. Some typical conditions that can produce roof leaks include the following:

◆ *Step flashing*—this is probably the most important requirement for sealing a roof structure. It is an age-old method of joining a roof surface where it meets a vertical wall; a pre-cut and bent piece of metal or other material is used to seal a joint from moisture where a sloping roof meets a wall, chimney, or other vertical surface. A small angular-shaped piece of metal is inserted between each over-lapping course of shingle (from the bottom to the top), sealed to the wall, and then counter-flashed.

◆ *Valley flashing*—a metal strip which runs the length of a valley, where shingles are not woven, in order to protect the structure where two roof planes come together or intersect.

◆ *Vent and skylight flashing*—usually consists of a combination of metal, rubber, or vinyl material designed specifically to protect joints where plumbing vents and skylights are installed at the roof surface.

◆ *Cricket or saddle*—a special-purpose flashing assembly designed to protect a structure from rainwater runoff and snow melt at the bottom run of a roof where it meets a chimney; such assemblies are generally made of metal and are sloped on two sides and made with a high vertical flange, which is caulked and attached to the surface of the chimney and crimped flashing (such as that of a valley flashing) which is installed under and extends well beyond the line of shingles.

◆ *Pitch pockets*—where posts and other supporting members are installed in a roof, proper installation is critical to the roof function. Posts must be set tightly in framing pockets that are properly caulked or sealed, flashing must then be installed at the roof surface prior to the installation of shingles or a membrane, and finally, counter-flashing must be set in a kerf cut in the post and caulked at the top and then installed and caulked over the existing flashing to insure a water-tight assembly.

◆ *Ice damming*—is a condition that may occur in gutters in areas subject to severe winter weather. In such cases, the repeated freeze and thaw creates a solid bed of ice in gutters and renders them ineffective. In rare cases where codes do not require back flashing at gutter boards, rainwater or snow melt may enter the structure by coming over the gutter board, into the soffit, and then into the structure. Unless gutter boards are flashed, ice damming will usually cause some interior damage unless gutters are removed as an emergency precaution or to relieve such a condition.

Wall Assembly Leaks—are leaks that relate to the vertical areas that create the envelope of a structure including gable ends, dormer walls, framed chimneys, window projections, and the like. Such leaks are often the result of inadequate flashing and caulking as follows:

◆ *Head flashing*—is metal (typically aluminum or copper) or vinyl flashing designed to prevent the downfall of storm water and snow from entering behind the top trim of a window, door, column, or other architectural detail.

◆ *Caulking*—to protect a structure from the adverse effects of water, moisture, or dampness, corner-boards, windows and doors must be carefully caulked using a high-grade caulking material; leaks can help cause decay, structural damage, and even damage to interior finishes and contents. Caulking is never an adequate substitute for proper flashing, but it must be used to seal trim elements, flashing, windows and doors from the adverse effects of weathering.

◆ *Water table*—is a protective ledge, molding, or string course along the vertical wall of a structure designed to throw off rainwater; wood siding and other trim elements are often set on top of a wood water table designed to act as a drip edge by forcing rainwater that sheets down the siding or trim element to fall to the ground and thus protect elements of the structure below it.

◆ *Window and door sill construction*—brick, stone, and concrete window and door sills must be installed with a slight slope in order to allow storm water and snow melt to drain away for the structure. In cases where the sill has no slope or a negative slope, caulking will eventually fail and allow moisture to enter or impact the structure. Where coursing may require a split under a window or door, a lazy mason, or a mason without the proper material may try to make a standard brick work; or perhaps it is the result of his ignorance or carelessness. Proper supervision and careful inspections are the only protection against this condition.

Foundation Leaks—are any leaks related to foundations or foundation drainage systems. Although all of the problems and conditions set forth above are important, none is more troublesome than a foundation leak. Where basements have been constructed, water will sometimes enter a finished, partially finished, or storage area and can create substantial embarrassment for a builder and his construction manager. As a professional, both the builder and his construction manager must be prepared to evaluate and deal with the consequences of a "basement leak." The following conditions may contribute to, or cause a wet basement or foundation leak:

◆ *Water table*—in this instance, the water table is the level or elevation below which the ground is saturated with water; the water table for a specific building site will vary depending on soils as well as seasonal conditions related to rainfall and snow melt. Prior to construction, the construction manager must have some idea where the approximate water table is; if he or she is building an in-ground basement below the water table, the foundation must be waterproofed and provide an effective method of keeping the basement dry.

◆ *Ground water*—is any water found below the earth's surface which may result from the water table, a spring, poor site grading, an unexplained source following a layer of rock in the subsoil, or, perhaps, water resulting from a leak in a nearby existing storm-drainage system. In any event, ground water is the most difficult of all basement-leak conditions to overcome because it is not always anticipated. It can cause hydrostatic pressure against foundation walls that can crack walls, cause weeping tie holes and mortar joints, and it can fill window wells to overflowing during rainstorms. Window well and foundation drainage systems are the primary sources for the relief of ground water. Most new homes with buried basements are built with window well drainage, an exterior foundation drainage system, and an interior under-slab drainage system that terminates in a sump. Where sumps are used, pumps will discharge any accumulated ground water; where ground water is substantial and requires almost continuous cycling, back-up pumps and a battery back-up electrical system should be installed either during house construction or, in the case of a condition that develops after completion, as a matter of proactive warranty service procedure after completion.

◆ *Site grading*—must provide adequate and positive drainage to remove surface water (including that generated by the roof of the structure) from the site during a storm event. Where grades around the structure do not allow storm water or snow melt to drain away from the structure, or in cases where ponding or puddling exists, ground water activity will increase.

◆ *Foundation drainage system*—may consist of both an exterior and/or an interior system. An exterior system typically consists of a three- or four-inch perforated pipe laid in a gravel bed, protected with a soil separator (on top) and drained to either a daylight discharge, or an interior sump with a pump. An interior system might consist of a perimeter (or grid) of three- or four-inch perforated pipe laid in a four-inch gravel bed under the slab that drains to an enclosed sump with a pit and pump for ejection.

By installing both an interior and exterior drainage system, the builder increases the possibilities for curing a ground water problem.

◆ *Window-well construction*—window wells without positive drains should provide adequate storage for water that may accumulate as rainfall or snow melt and perhaps some storage capacity to offset slight ground water conditions. Wells without positive drainage systems are usually constructed with a column of coarse gravel that will provide storage for 8 to 10 gallons of water. In some cases, where dampproofing is adequate and positive drainage is not available, a builder may hold the gravel down six to eight inches from the window sill and install two or more three-foot sections of four-inch perforated pipe with caps in order to increase the potential to displace ground water. In cases where there is a substantial ground water condition and no exterior drainage is available, but interior drainage exists, it may become necessary to install a relief drain just below the window sill using a PVC pipe that can be brought through the foundation wall, turned inside the wall, and extended through the slab to the under-slab drainage system; this solution should be used only as a last resort because it brings outside ground water inside and may require more frequent pump operation. Window wells will have a tendency to fill when grades away from a downspout are inadequate and allow rainwater to settle at the foundation; this condition will also allow the poorly compacted backfill around a foundation to settle and exacerbate problems related to poor drainage around the house.

◆ *Dampproofing and waterproofing*—dampproofing is any process used to prevent light moisture from penetrating a building material or structure; waterproofing is any process used to prevent water from entering a building material or structure. Dampproofing retards dampness or water penetration under non-hydrostatic pressure due to capillary action in construction material while waterproofing prevents water under hydrostatic pressure from entering the structure. Unless they are building on a site with a high water table or a considerable amount of ground water, most builders will use one or more coats of bituminous foundation coat, over a poured concrete wall or a Portland cement applied to unit masonry walls. Some will use cement coatings, bonding mortars, acrylic latex coatings, or 6 mil polyethylene sheeting to achieve better results, but waterproofing requires the use of water tight membrane materials. Such materials may be either built up on the job-site or installed using separate sheet materials designed for that purpose such as butyl rubber, EPDM, neoprene, or Hypalon (chlorosulfonated polyethylene) that are bonded to the wall with adhesives. Bitumen should not be applied when outdoor temperatures are at or near freezing and footings should be clean and dry in order to seal the joint between the footing and wall.

◆ *Gutters and downspout drainage*—the impact of roof drainage must not be overlooked by a service technician or others trying to evaluate the cause of a foundation leak or flooding window wells; water that is not collected by poorly maintained gutters will have a substantial effect on the volume of ground water and a single downspout often carries the drainage from 20 percent or more of a roof structure.

◆ *Tie hole and service entrance leaks*—where such leaks develop, it is generally the result of ground water around the foundation; ground water often finds a weak spot such as a tie hole or water service entrance; ground water will generally find its way into the newly compacted backfill of a utility trench. These leaks can generally be repaired easily by removing some of the material around the tie hole or utility line, replacing it with hydraulic cement, and covering the patch with a skin of roofers caulk.

◆ *Brick ledge and water leaks*—in cases where a brick ledge has been buried below grade, water can sometimes move along the ledge to window or door openings, or to window wells. It is not uncommon to find this condition where weep holes have been buried thoughtlessly.

Any water problem in a completed house should be treated as an emergency and such complaints should be evaluated while the leak is active. It takes skill to evaluate a water problem and set the direction to resolve a complicated foundation leak. Any evaluation must progress from one area of concern to another until all bases have been covered and the picture becomes clear:

◆ *Gutters and downspouts* must be clean and functioning. Downspouts must be clear and the resulting discharge must move away from the foundation.

◆ *Drainage* must be positive and move stormwater around the structure and off-site. There must be no areas of long-term (more than 48 hours after the storm event) ponding, or puddling and there should be no obvious depressions from the settlement of utility-line ditches which would allow water to course back to the foundation. Here it is important to note window well conditions because they may indicate the volume of ground water at the foundation or perhaps they have not been properly constructed with enough volume to displace normal stormwater.

◆ *Sump conditions*—checking a sump will help evaluate whether or not the existing drainage system is performing properly. An under-slab drainage system will generally relieve high ground water or water that has followed a sewer line; a drainage system that combines exterior foundation drainage and under-slab drainage will also relieve ground water that has found its way to the foundation wall. An evaluation of the volume of activity in the sump will indicate the condition relative to the storm in progress. In order to properly evaluate such conditions, it is sometimes necessary to inspect the sump several days following a storm event in order to rule out water-table activity.

◆ *General interior conditions*—include the specific complaint, the volume of water present, and any emergency measures that may have been taken to mitigate the problem. Sometimes it is helpful to know if any construction has occurred in the immediate area that may have had an impact on ground water or drainage.

The best way to deal with a potential wet-basement problem is to start during the feasibility period. Know where the water table is; understand the porosity, permeability, and capillarity characteristics of existing soils; identify rock; and then design the best drainage and protection system to insure a dry basement for your purchaser. Nothing can produce more ill will than a water leak and where a construction manager is not sure of the success of his or her efforts, he or she may want to give the homeowner a pager number, or perhaps his home phone number, as an indication of good faith.

SOLUTION

All water leaks should be considered an emergency condition and taken ahead of normal day-to-day service activity.

OTHER POST-CLOSING COMPLAINTS

Other less sensitive, but nevertheless important complaints that follow closing include a broad range of topics.

Squeaks and Deflection

Floor squeaks are the leading callback and represent a substantial cost for service departments around the country. After construction is complete, builders and their service technicians can only make simple repairs where floor systems are unfinished below or they must remove ceiling coverings and pull back carpet, find the joist alignment, open the floor, place glue in hangers, install cleats, and then screw down sub-flooring in order to help quiet deep squeaks. In order to affect a cure for this condition, builders and their construction managers would be well advised to look at construction details and specifications for a preventive solution; understand the causes of deflection and cure them in the plan or in the material specification. Consider the following conditions in order to reduce such unnecessary callbacks:

◆ Carefully consider the spans, spacing, sizing, and quality (including the species of wood) of the framing material required by the plans and specifications, and then adjust it wherever necessary in order to eliminate undesirable deflection.

◆ Confirm the nailing schedules and application of adhesives during construction, in order to maintain the integrity of the fastening system.

◆ Assign the specific responsibility of inspecting and reinforcing sub-floor and underlayment prior to the framing inspection in order to strengthen the floors prior to the application of finishes. Some builders will either use screws to fasten deck sheathing, or they will reinforce wood decks by selectively screwing sub-floor as required, and then screwing down underlayment when a ceramic or marble tile covering is to be used; this is easily accomplished using a belt-fed screw gun with a coarsely threaded screw.

◆ Use solid blocking in lieu of wood or metal bridging where sub-flooring is glued and nailed. This will generally produce a more rigid floor system with slightly less deflection.

◆ Conducting conscientious inspections prior to concealment in order to identify areas of unusual deflection or noise.

◆ Remind homeowners that some minor squeaks are normal and may occur from time-to-time depending on the level of humidity in the house.

Plumb, Square, and Level

Most homeowners are under the impression that walls are always built plumb and square, and that floors are level. In fact, slight variances exist and, in most cases, never become an issue unless they are extreme; adjusting finishes such as trim, ceramic tile, floor coverings, and wallpaper to allow for such slight variances is not a normal requirement according to industry standards. By splitting the error created by a slightly more severe condition, the result may just produce a condition that is acceptable under the standard, not noticeable to the eye, and dos not affect the overall quality of the construction.

In cases where such variances are noticeable or extreme, they must be reckoned with, and often cause considerable disappointment to homeowners after completion. A homeowner will generally only complain about a wall being out of plumb or square, or a floor out of level, if it is noticeable and, therefore, an extensive repair may become necessary after occupancy. Most home builders will remedy such conditions when they are noticeable to the eye, or where they exceed industry standards. In order to avoid this costly condition, a conscientious project manager will:

◆ Check the elevations of footings and foundation walls carefully. In most cases where a concrete foundation wall is used, the wall will be level if the footings are level; where block walls are used, top-of-wall elevations must be checked carefully before framing begins and plates may need to be shimmed to adjust for minor variations.

◆ Spot check all walls using a long level and straight edge prior to concealment; wood-framed interior walls can often be adjusted slightly by driving a block against a top or bottom plate with a sledge hammer.

◆ Spot check walls for square by placing a large framing square on inside corners at top and bottom plates; wood-framed interior walls may then be adjusted by driving them with a sledge hammer as outlined above.

◆ Pull string lines across interior slabs before framing where depressions are suspected.

◆ Be very careful to insure that the depth of all floor and wall framing material is compatible and that adjustments have been made for shrinkage in cases where solid lumber has been used with engineered wood products in floor construction.

Ceramic Tile Damage

Two of the most common warranty repairs to ceramic tile result from line cracking and the separation of tiles from backers at tub and shower walls. Line cracking generally results from poorly installed sub-floor and/or underlayment, or unusual deflection in floor trusses or joists; in most cases, sub-flooring and underlayment has not been properly glued, nailed, and/or screwed, or deflection may occur as a result of inadequate strength, defective material, or improper installation. Where line cracking occurs, the tiles are generally removed, an inspection is made of the structural elements in the floor system, reinforcing is installed wherever possible, existing underlayment is screwed down, and replacement tiles are installed and grouted. Tile separation at tub and shower walls is generally due to the deterioration of the tile backer which may result from moisture produced by inadequate caulking, a plumbing leak, or wicking which has occurred where the backer has been extended into the shower pan. Construction managers will try to avoid this problem by using a high-quality tile backer designed for high moisture areas, by caulking all tub and shower walls during punch-out in preparation for closing, and by inspecting tile backer after installation to be sure that it does not extend into a shower pan. Where separation has occurred, one or more courses of tile and the damaged backer must be removed, new backer must be installed, and replacement tiles (from the same run) are then installed and grouted. In both cases, such warranty work can generally be prevented by: (1) developing rigid floor systems, (2) enforcing standard fastening systems and nailing schedules, (3) using high-quality water resistant tile backer, (4) making the drywall contractor responsible to hold the tile backer two inches above the shower drain or using a pre-molded shower receptor, and (5) making oversight inspections of such conditions during construction.

Carpet Re-stretching
All wall-to-wall carpets will become loose in high traffic areas and, although some carpets will perform better than others, they all generally require re-stretching. In order to avoid responsibility issues with owners, contractors, and subcontractors, all contracts with vendors who furnish and install wall-to-wall carpeting should include a provision for one free re-stretch during the first year of occupancy. This will serve to acknowledge the responsibility of the subcontractor and create a routine solution for the homeowner; homeowners should be instructed at the time of the walk-through inspection to schedule this service anytime within the first year at their convenience.

Repairing Finished Surfaces
During the finish stage of construction, surfaces must be protected from the potential damage related to normal construction activity. In addition to the ordinary care which must be taken by tradesmen and helpers, alert managers will see to it that pre-finished materials such as cabinets and vanities are masked, they will use temporary covers to protect bath tubs, and they will use pressure-sensitive adhesive-backed polyethylene film and drop-cloths to protect carpeting, tops, and other finished surfaces. In spite of such efforts, finished surfaces may be scratched, chipped, or otherwise damaged prior to delivery or during warranty service work. In these cases, the damaged surfaces must be repaired and restored to a high-quality finish as quickly as possible. Both punch-out and service technicians must be trained to use touchup kits for pre-finished cabinets, vanities, and flooring; to point-up and touchup damaged drywall finishes; to use putty and caulking material to repair damaged trim; to use chemical cleaners to clean brass and other surfaces; to use marble waxes and furniture polish to restore the luster of some surfaces; and to coordinate professional repairs when they are required. Professionals can successfully repair most construction damage that may occur to marble, cultured marble, laminate surfaces, porcelain, fiberglass, ceramic tile, carpet, wallpaper, and similar specialty surfaces.

In order to prevent unnecessary concern for such repairs, they should be made quickly; if the repair is completed properly, the surface will be restored to its original condition and perform satisfactorily. Where such damage occurs in the course of a warranty repair, the homeowner must be reassured that the repair will be made by a professional, that it will be guaranteed by the builder, and that it will restore the surface to its original condition. Most homeowners will cooperate and accept a repair in lieu of replacement providing that the surface is restored to its original condition. In cases where carpeting has only been slightly damaged by clean water, it is common for builders to use a professional to dry, sanitize, and shampoo the carpet rather than replace it; in most cases, that means fans to air dry prior to normal shampoo and sanitizing efforts.

Dust, Dirt, and Service Process

Dust control and proper clean-up procedures are critical to the success of any warranty service program. Too often, home builders will use inexperienced tradesmen to perform routine post-settlement warranty service work and much of what they do is related to drywall repairs and paint touch up. Unless these technicians are trained and understand the importance of dust control and the need for protecting the homeowner's property, they will become the subject of ongoing complaints.

SOLUTION

Apply solutions to these complaints that are fair and reasonable and enjoy the results. Use experienced technicians or train your service staff to understand the importance of dust control, the need to protect the homeowner's property, and the need to cleanup when they finish for the day. Provide them with the necessary dust screens, drop cloths, masking tape, and a vacuum cleaner with a fine particle filter . . . this action should at least reduce such complaints.

CHAPTER 7

SPECIFIC RESPONSES
TO SPECIFIC COMPLAINTS

The following is a list of statements that you might hear from customers and responses that would be typical in a company with a proactive customer care department. The statements might come from any customer and should be accepted without regard for how they might grade your performance. Every customer should be extended the same level of compassion, respect, and customer care. Some experienced men and women who deal with customer service on a daily basis think of it as a non-emotional process that requires professional responses and follow-up—regardless of the conditions; they are confident in their abilities to minimize the loss of goodwill and to protect the company in the case of arbitration, litigation, or media involvement.

SALES PROCESS

"We have been waiting for two months and your company still has not started the house. We are very concerned that we will not make the school start in September if you don't get started."

It sounds like a permit delay, but let me check our internal schedule. Yes, we had to re-site the house, which took us a week and then submitted for the permit five weeks ago. The county is taking a little longer than usual to process permits right now because of the volume of applications. Let me call and see where we are, and I will have Jim [your sales manager] get back to you.

"We just got our Non-Standard Option request back and we cannot believe the price you have given us. I looked at similar cabinets at Home Store and they are much cheaper."

I am sorry you are disappointed, but our pricing is based on standard mark-ups for the industry. We survey our competition and establish our rates, based on what we feel is a fair, reasonable, and competitive position. Keep in mind that we are home builders, that the material specifications are not the same, and that we're trying to accommodate your request.

"We just bought Lot 27 and we want a conventional fireplace for the living room and master bedroom. The house is currently being framed and we were told by the Sales Manager that we could not get it."

I am sorry you are disappointed, but Brian is right. To maintain control of our process, all structural options must be selected before the start of construction. If you would like a gas fireplace for your master bedroom, we may still be able to get one on a Non-Standard Option if we move quickly [say no, but offer a compromise].

CLOSINGS

"Can you tell me when your company intends to deliver my house? My family is living out of suitcases in a motel, the house is essentially finished, and we have heard nothing from you regarding settlement."

Oh my, I can certainly see why you are anxious to move in. Let me see what I can find out? [checking the internal report] According to our internal construction schedule, the Project Manager expects to have the house ready for Orientation early next month and you could probably settle the following week if everything else is in order. Let me talk to Jane Smith, our Settlement Coordinator, and see if we are prepared to confirm these dates and send you a settlement notification.

"I just stopped to see our new house and the carpet they installed in the living room is the wrong grade and color."

"Well, that certainly must have been a surprise. Will you be in your office this afternoon; I would like to check into it and then, either I will call you back or I will have your Sales Manager get back to you." [This can only occur as a result of a company or contractor error, or the buyer has made a mistake; the documents and a verification from your contractor will give you the answer.]

"I am very upset. We just came from our Orientation and the house was filthy, unfinished, has missing parts, and we are scheduled to settle next week."

Let me begin by saying that we will get involved at the highest level and work directly with you until your settlement is complete, in order to help you feel more comfortable. If what you say is accurate, I don't blame you for being upset. It sounds like we've made a big mistake. Our policy is not to present or deliver a new home that is not finished, and it certainly has to be a disappointment for you and your family to see your new home in such a condition. Will you give me a chance to get involved; I would like to get the facts and have our Vice President of Construction call you this afternoon.

"We are getting ready to go to settlement, but we have a great big problem. There is a large drainage swale in our backyard and your Sales Manager told us that the Company would probably be willing to give us a credit of $2,000 if we accepted it, but a credit memo has never been issued." [this has been a very aggressive purchaser with a history of unreasonable demands]

Well, let's see what we can find out. Can you hold while I get Beverly [the Sales Manager] on the phone with us?

"We are getting ready to settle and there are three large items missing including the shower door in the master bath, the canister for the central vacuum system, and the landscaping. We refuse to go to settlement without these items or a substantial escrow."

I am sorry we were unable to complete these items, Jim. I was in the house yesterday and I know the house was in great shape with these exceptions. I understand that the shower door arrived late and had to be taken back to the shop to be re-cut; the contractor says that he will install it tomorrow. The canister for the central vac is on backorder, and we should have it next week. Unfortunately, the landscaping will have to wait until this rain stops and the ground dries out; I'm sure we'll be able to have everything completed sometime next week. I think it would be unreasonable for you not to go to settlement, the loan documents have been prepared, your contract anticipates some open items, and you are scheduled for this afternoon. I understand your disappointment, but we cannot escrow funds. Why don't you let me send over a letter of acknowledgment with my assurance as the Director of Construction that we will complete these items as quickly as possible; if this works for you, I'll check in with you next week and stay with you until the work is complete.

"I'm angry. I just received word that I will not be able to settle on my new house tomorrow morning because you failed the final inspection yesterday and will not have my occupancy permit until Friday. My mover is scheduled for tomorrow, I have to be out of my old house, and I have no idea what I am supposed to do with my family and a large dog. I know you are a Vice President and I appreciate the fact that you have been trying to get in touch with me, but this is unexpected and I'm pissed off."

Carl, please let me start by apologizing. I can see that this situation has created considerable disappointment and frustration for you. At a time when you should be looking forward to the excitement of your new home, you're forced to manage a crisis. What we thought would be a routine inspection resulted in a failure because a new inspector is requiring a different configuration on the vent for your water heater. This seems a little unfair to us, but we have no choice but to comply. We've made arrangements for the modification tomorrow and a re-inspection early Friday morning. I spoke with the County Building Department and they have given me permission to let you move your furniture in the house tomorrow, but you cannot stay in the house overnight. We will need a standard storage agreement, but that should be no problem for you. I would like to make arrangements for you and your family to spend the night at the XYZ Hotel; the lodging would be at our expense. Do you have someone who will take your dog overnight?

CONSTRUCTION

"I can't believe that it has taken your company four months to get my house ready for trim and you are still telling me that it will take another six weeks until settlement. What am I supposed to do about the people who have bought my house?"

I'm sorry things haven't moved along a little better for us, I know you are frustrated and so are we. The County took six weeks to approve your building permit, we've had something like twelve days of rain, and now, the power company has delayed us. It's a complicated process. More than seventy-five trade contractors and suppliers have to be coordinated in addition to the public utilities. That's why we constantly remind you not to rely too heavily on our internal schedule. Do you remember what I told you when we had our Pre-Construction Meeting; how difficult it was to predict the final delivery date in such an active market with such a shortage of labor? You know we will try to improve the schedule, but a cannot promise it. What can I do to help? [unfortunately, you know that there is probably nothing you can do, but if you don't ask, you may miss a legitimate opportunity to help . . . it may be as simple as a letter to his buyer.]

"I am an engineer and I believe that the steel beam supporting the house is undersized. It should be heavier and I want it changed."

A structural engineer reviews our architectural plans before they are finalized and they are then submitted to the County for review. We should be in good shape, but I will have a structural engineer review the condition and I will send you a copy of his report for your file. [Keep in mind that it would not be unusual to discover a legitimate problem this way; this purchaser may be giving you some good advice.]

"I left you a list on your trailer door with 12 issues that I have with the construction of the house. I went through it on Monday evening and made the list, but I have heard nothing from you."

I received the list and I promise you I will be sure that the items are covered before we close the house in. As I mentioned in our Pre-Construction Meeting, our policy is not to respond to such lists; we note them and put them in the file, but we do not respond. The fact is that your house in a work in process and I'm well aware of its condition. When we get the house ready for drywall, I will contact you and walk the house with you in order to discuss the rough structure and give you an opportunity to see it before concealment. The items on your list are not unusual and I promise you I will deal with them prior to your Pre-Drywall Walk. In addition, we have municipal inspections, and I am required to complete an 80- to 90-item checklist prior to drywall; it's part of the internal Quality Assurance Program that I mentioned at our Pre-Construction Meeting.

"When I was in the house over the weekend, I noticed a crack in the concrete foundation wall and I am concerned."

You're right, Frank. I noticed it last Friday and called a structural engineer to make an inspection. I think the wall may have been damaged during backfill, but I am not sure. If I'm right, we'll have a contractor inject the crack with an epoxy; it's a standard repair in such cases, the wall will be stronger at the crack than it was originally, and the contractor will provide us with both a certification and an additional warranty on his work. I'll give Jim [the Sales Manager] a copy of the report for you when I get it. [this is a good example of setting expectations].

"I was out over the weekend and it looks like the house is in the wrong spot. It looks too close to the road and I am concerned about the large tree in the front yard; it may not make it."

Let me take a look at it and discuss it with the construction manager. I will get back to you and if you are still uncomfortable, we can get Ben [the construction manager] to meet with us early one morning. Will you be in your office tomorrow morning?

"I am calling you because I know you're the Director of Construction and I am upset with your Project Manager at Fairfax Station. I used to think he was a good man, but I now have my doubts. Every time I approach Bob, he becomes defensive, impatient, sometimes, down right, rude. I don't like him and I don't want to have to deal with him.

Well, this doesn't sound good. I'm sorry our ability to support you hasn't been better. I am surprised. Bob has been with the company for five years, he has a great reputation . . . there must be six or eight letters from homeowners in his file for outstanding service. I think he is probably under a great deal of pressure right now; he has 20 homes under construction, he has 6 more to start, and I know he has to deliver 5 this month. Unless I'm mistaken, the next time you see Bob will be at your Orientation. Until then, I'll try to help coordinate things with you. How can I help?

"I was in my house last night and I noticed some mold on the party wall between my house and the house next door and I am concerned."

I understand. We're aware that mold is a sensitive issue and we monitor the website of the American Lung Association and are currently working with both the Northern Virginia Building Industry Association and the Loudoun County Building Department on this issue. Mold on construction sites is largely the result of rainy, damp weather . . . and it loves gypsum party wall material. Just before insulating the house, we inspect party walls for mold and, where it is present, we wash the walls down with a solution of water and bleach, let it dry, and wash it down again. After the second bleach solution has dried, we will then spray the affected areas with a primer that kills mildew in order to seal the area. This is the prescribed treatment in such cases. If you want more information, you can call the County Health Department, I can give you the number if you'd like.

"I want to have a home inspector accompany me on my Orientation. What is your position?"

You have the right to have a third-party inspector make an inspection if you wish, as long as it is an inspector that we have approved in advance [this is also a point covered in the contract of sale]. Although we feel that it is an unnecessary expense, we certainly recognize that some buyers are more comfortable with such an inspection. The only reason that we would deny an inspector is if we had a history of unprofessional performance. If you would like to send me an email with your inspectors name and the company that he represents, I will reply immediately for the record.

"This is Mrs. Schwartz. I received a call from Ken [the Sales Manager] yesterday and he advised me that our ceramic tile selection was not available and that the contractor had made a substitution without our approval. This is unacceptable and I am upset about it. We had planned our whole decorating scheme around that tile."

I apologize for your disappointment, but maybe we can resolve the matter in some acceptable way. Our policy and the contractor's scope of work clearly states that in the event that a substitution becomes necessary, the purchaser will be consulted in advance. We expect some reasonable resolution, but we do not want our contractors to make such a substitution unless we direct them to do so. Let me confirm the conditions and I will get back to you this afternoon. Will you be at your home number? [The company is already aware of the circumstances and has a call in to the contractor; he must either replace the floor with an approved substitute or pick-up the discount in the event that the company can successfully negotiate one with the purchaser.]

"You're the President of this stupid company and I expect some action. I have told everyone that I will not accept your conclusion that I didn't pay for a gas fireplace upgrade in the master bedroom and I am not entitled to it; you have it in the model and you are going to give it to me at no cost. You are all a bunch of #x@ holes and if you think you are going to #@#% with me, you are crazy . . . I'll get an attorney!

Tom, I want to discuss this with you and try to help, but it's clear to me that you are far too emotional right now. I would like to suggest that we discuss this later today after you have had a chance to calm down. If you would prefer that I discuss this situation with your attorney, I'm more than willing to accommodate you, but I would like an opportunity to discuss it further with you when you calm down. Will you be available around 4:00 today? [Regardless of the outcome, the President will send a letter by close of business in order to document the behavior.]

"My wife and I just completed our Orientation and had over 50 items on our list related to paint, drywall, and trim. I was surprised that the house wasn't in better shape, I thought you guys had a reputation for quality construction."

I'm sorry we didn't meet your expectations. We have a quality assurance program that includes a "manager's walk" that is designed to screen our homes prior to the presentation to our customers. A senior manager inspects every house before it is presented. I'm sure that one of our managers inspected your house prior to presentation. Fit and finish, in any price range, is a matter of reasonable standards in the market. We purchase high-quality materials and we try to use the best tradesmen available. Unfortunately, we sometimes fail to meet the expectations of our purchasers, but in every case, we will work hard to overcome your objection. I'm sure that Jim [the construction manager] will make every reasonable effort to improve things for you.

"The brick color on my house doesn't look anything like the sample in the decorator center."

I had heard that you were concerned about the color and I checked to confirm that the brick that our contractor installed was, in fact, the brick that you selected. Unfortunately, there are slight variations in every run; brick, tile, carpeting, and some other materials are subject to slight variations that occur during the production process. Do you feel that the color variation is significant? [If the answer is affirmative, the company will have it inspected by an independent third-party, and then consider the possibility of a field coloring process applied by a specialty contractor at the expense of the manufacturer if necessary.]

"The granite top installed in my kitchen looks nothing like the top sample in the model."

I'm sorry you are disappointed. Granite is a natural material with considerable variations. That's why we insist that our purchasers inspect the slab before the top is cut and polished. Did you not have that opportunity? [In fact, he was extended the opportunity and declined it; the time and date of the conversation was recorded and placed in the file.]

"I am totally frustrated with your building process. I sometimes wonder if you guys know what you're doing."

How can I help restore your confidence? [This sends a signal that you are willing to listen and sincerely want to provide a service. It will also draw out the cause of the frustration and provide the employee an opportunity to deal with a specific concern.]

SETTLEMENT

"My walls are damaged at the stairs to the second floor and at the doorway to the basement, you need to repair and paint them."

[After seeing the damage and with a smile, the Warranty Service Technician responds.] That's mover damage that isn't covered by your warranty . . . but I will take care of it while I'm here as a courtesy. [When he finishes, he makes a note of it and has the homeowner initial it for the file.]

"Can you send Tom by to see me? I'm having a problem with my gutters. Every time it rains, water pours over the edge and the downspouts are not working."

It sounds to me like your gutters need to be cleaned. How long ago did you have them cleaned? [Keep in mind that there is an outside possibility that the gutters may have been set with an improper pitch or somehow damaged in the finishing process.] This is not a warranty item; it is normal maintenance work. Can I help by giving you the name of an independent contractor who does this type of work? [Always try to offer a solution. Often, homeowners just need to know where to get help.]

"We moved into our home two weeks ago and we just noticed two large stains in the carpet in our living room. These stains are not ours and we want our carpet replaced."

Well, let's see if we can figure out what's happened. Were the stains in the carpet at the time of your Orientation? [Regardless of the response, the story goes on] I will send a technician out to take a look at the stains; we may be able to remove them for you. If not, we may ask a company that specializes in carpet analysis to make an inspection and analyze the stains to determine what created them and what we can do about safely removing them.

"I have a large pool of water that stands in the back corner of my house and I want you to do something about it. My children can't use this area after it rains."

Is it wet right now? [Yes it rained over night and my yard is a mess.] In general, the standard for standing water is whether or not it drains over a 48-hour period. I think Joe will be in your area tomorrow; I will have him stop and make an inspection. Will you be home in the morning? [Joe will make a visual inspection, take pictures, and file a report.]

"I moved into my new house two months ago and my yard looks terrible. The sod is dieing, there must have been something wrong with it. I have been watering it."

Tom will be in your area Friday, I will have him make an inspection and get back to you early nest week. It's been very hot over the past four weeks, how often have you been watering it and how long have you soaked it. [Three times a week for about a half hour; I move the sprinkler around]. Well, that might not be enough, but let 's look at it, there are ways of determining what is happening. Generally, if a yard is under-watered in hot weather, new sod will shrink and open gaps between the edges. I'll get back to you the first of the week. [In fact, the sod had drawn up on the edges; a common swale with the house next door was healthy because the neighbor had kept his lawn watered. Pictures were taken, a report was completed for the file, and the company made an offer in writing to have the yard replaced at cost for the purchaser. The Superintendent had put a door hanger on the house five weeks earlier warning the homeowner to keep the yard watered, the company provided watering instructions in the Orientation package, and the Service Technician had covered the topic at the Orientation.]

"I want to arrange for a service appointment so you can finish a list of items on my house."

[The Customer Care Coordinator recognizes this homeowner as a very difficult customer with a long history of abusive behavior.] Mary, can you hold just a minute while I pull your file? [Yes.] I see that you settled fourteen months ago and we have already completed six lists . . . your year-end work was completed and signed off by you in July. [Continued demand for attention.] Why don't you fax your list to my attention and I'll discuss it with our Vice President and get back to you tomorrow? [This will give the company an opportunity to see the new list of the complaints and decide whether to draw the line at that point, or to continue over-servicing for the record. This is a decision that only the Vice President can make.]

"I apologize for calling you at home, but I didn't know what else to do. It's Thanksgiving morning, I have 12 people coming for dinner, and water is pouring through every opening in my ceilings; my hardwood floors are ruined, we have buckets everywhere, and I am about to have a heart attack."

Jim, do you have any idea what has caused it? [Yes, your construction manager had men working on my roof yesterday and they didn't finish. They put a piece of plastic over the area they opened and the wind has blown it back.] You woke me up and it will take me a few minutes to dress, but I will get there as soon as possible; I'm 40 minutes from your house, but I will leave in the next 10 minutes. Please try to relax if you can, the company accepts full responsibility, and I promise you that I will get things under control for you. [The homeowners were entirely reasonable people. The Vice President of Construction who answered this call, sent the family and their guests to dinner at a fine country restaurant with a great reputation, he was able to stop the flow of water, and contain the drainage process by driving holes in the drywall ceiling and catching the water in buckets. It was the worse condition that the young Vice President had ever experienced, but he managed to find solutions. In conversation, he learned that Jim had to be in Texas for a week-long meeting beginning the next day and Martha was a mother of two small children and didn't work. He was able to convince Jim to take Martha with him to Texas for the week, take the children and any small valuables to her mothers for the week, and give him a key to the house and the week to put things back in order. Even though the condition had resulted from a construction manager's poor judgment and failure to properly supervise the roof repair, this couple gave him a gift when they returned to what must have seemed like a new house.]

"Your Service Technician was working in my house this morning. I caught him looking in my nightstand and when I confronted him, he denied it. I have no idea what he was looking for, but I have thrown him out. After he left, I found that my pistol was missing, and I think I should call the cops."

Joe, this doesn't sound right. Bob has been with the company for six years, has a great reputation, and I would be surprised if he would even touch your pistol. I suppose that you have to do what you think is best. I will contact Bob now and have him return to your house to meet with the police if you would like. [No, I don't want him anywhere near my house.] Well, I will talk to Bob immediately and get back to you, please give the police my name and phone number and I will coordinate with them. [Bob alleges that he was merely moving a night table and opened the drawer in order to get a handhold. When questioned about the pistol he denied it and offered to take a polygraph test. Following his interview with the Vice President, a summary was placed in the file and the VP called the homeowner and told him that he believed Bob and that Bob would be willing to take a polygraph test. Two hours later, the homeowner called to let everyone know that he had found his misplaced pistol.]

"We're uncomfortable. It's 95° outside and I can't get my house cool. It's 82° in my master bedroom and 80° in my living room. Last week, I called in and your contractor came to the house, made some adjustments, and told me we should be fine. What do we do now?"

Well, let's see if we can't get to the bottom of this. You told me last week that your thermostats were both set at 72° and that you don't move them, is that correct? [That's right.] Last week, our contractor balanced the system thinking the problem was air - low between rooms. Let me explain the evaluation process so you will understand what must be done now. Your system has been designed to maintain an average room-to-room indoor temperature of 75° with an outside temperature of 95°. To understand what's happening, we will have to evaluate the conditions, including insulation, the equipment performance, and the distribution of air.

1. Temperatures should be in the 90s again tomorrow and I will have our Production Manager for that area call you and stop in to shoot temperatures around the house; he will use a device that will give him instant temperature readings on walls, ceilings, at supply and return registers, and in each room at chest high. He will record this information along with the outdoor temperature at the front door and file a written inspection report. This information will help us understand what's going on, whether we have an insulation problem, a distribution problem, or a system problem.
2. Assuming that it is a system problem, we will then ask our contractor to make a detailed evaluation and issue a written report. They will check the calibration of the thermostat; they will confirm the input and output of the equipment in order to be assured that it meets the manufacturers specifications; they will evaluate the ductwork and airflow at both the supplies and returns in order to confirm air volume and distribution; and they will conduct their own room-to-room temperature evaluation.
3. In the unlikely event that there are no irregularities with the equipment or distribution system, they will then go back and evaluate the original engineering calculations, but I have to tell you that we have built six other models like yours in the community and we have no other complaints.

Does this sound like a reasonable approach to you? [The problem turned out to be a crushed supply duct to the master bedroom on the upper level system, and a return on the first floor that had been covered with drywall (not cut-out and trimmed) in the finishing process. Both embarrassing conditions for which the company sent a dinner certificate with a letter of apology with a copy to the trade contractor.]

"Your company sent two drywall finishers into my home this morning to make some repairs. Your service technician left them unsupervised and when I got home this afternoon, they had drywall dust over my entire first floor. I have a number of valuable art objects, oriental carpets, and antique furniture. Everything is a mess and I am pissed off! You are the Vice President in charge and I would suggest that you get involved immediately."

You are absolutely right. Are you home now? [Yes.] I will leave the office in the next five minutes and I will be there in the next half hour. I completely understand your frustration and concern and I promise you that we will restore things to their original condition immediately. I am embarrassed that we would do such a thing, but we accept full responsibility and I will do everything I can to minimize your inconvenience. I'll see you shortly. [The homeowner is an attorney who just moved into a $900 thousand-dollar house, he has extraordinary furnishings, and has been fair and reasonable throughout the process. While in rout, the Vice President mobilized a five-man crew of high-end house cleaners and told them to bring vacuums with fine particle filters. After providing reasonable assurances to the homeowner, he sent them out to dinner at the company's expense and the cleaning crew had completed the clean-up by the time they returned at 10:00 PM.]

"Every time it rains, I get water in my basement. I've reported it four times and you have still done nothing to correct it. I want my foundation waterproofed and my yard regarded or I will sue your company . . . you're the owner and you're ignoring me."

Sid, I have never ignored you. I have made three inspections myself and in spite of the fact that you continue to send us letters that describe a wet basement, we have never seen any water in your basement. I have an unlisted home phone number, but I gave it to you and you have called me late in the evening on three occasions to complain of water in your basement. In every case, I have made an inspection personally and found no water; on the last two occasions, I even photographed the conditions for the record. You continue to send me letters describing a wet basement, and I continue to send you letters with copies of inspection reports that indicate that there is no problem. My question is why are you doing this; what have we done to deserve this kind of behavior? [The response here is immaterial.] This company has tried in vein to provide proactive service and maintain your goodwill, but you continue to aggressively pursue litigation, and I am at a loss to understand why. This is the second home that this company has built for you. At this point, I like you to consider taking this dispute to arbitration. [This is based on a true story that resulted in homeowner litigation that was subsequently dropped at the suggestion of a mediator who just happened to be a circuit court judge, in a pretrial conference.]

"I was told by your Vice President that my house was out of warranty and that you will not respond to my requests for additional service. This house is very poorly built, you refuse to give me reasonable service, and that's not acceptable. As the owner of the company, you should know that your Vice President is rude, lazy, and doesn't even return calls. I want satisfaction or I will picket your model home and go to the press . . . I have a friend who writes for the Gazette."

Barbara, I am sorry that we haven't met your expectations. Our experience tells us that Jim is an excellent employee and that he works hard to provide an exceptional

level of customer care. I am certain that we have nothing to hide; if you would like us to speak to the press, we are fully prepared. If you decide to picket our model home, please know that we will consider such an action an unfair attack on the company and hold you accountable for your actions. [The owner periodically audits the lot files and monitors the files on difficult customers; he is certain that Jim has done an excellent job of following policy. He knows the history of this customer and is satisfied that the documentation necessary to defeat her is in the file. *He also knows how important it is to protect those who have the misfortune to be responsible for the management of this group of tough customers.*]

struction managers and customer care directors, coordinators, and technicians should be familiar with building standards in order to clearly understand what constitutes defective construction. Some of the more notable standards that establish minimum conditions of acceptable construction include the following:

CONCRETE

◆ Foundations should not exceed ½" out of level in 20', with no ridge or depression in excess of ¼" in any 32" measurement.

◆ Foundation walls should not be more than 1" out of level over the entire surface and not vary more than ½" out of square when measured along a diagonal of 6' × 8' × 10' in any corner.

◆ Cracks in foundation walls greater than ⅛" in width are considered excessive, and cracks in excess of ¼" are unacceptable.

◆ Cracks in flatwork exceeding ³⁄₁₆" in width or ⅛" in vertical displacement are considered excessive.

◆ Cracks in garage slabs in excess of ¼" in width or ¼" in vertical displacement are unacceptable.

◆ Floors in rooms designed for habitability should not have pits, depressions, or areas of unevenness exceeding ¼" in any 32" measurement.

◆ Water should drain from stoops and steps.

MASONRY

◆ Cracks greater than ⅛" in width are considered excessive, and cracks in excess of ¼" are unacceptable.

◆ Foundations should not exceed ½" out of level in 20' with no ridge or depression in excess of ¼" within any 32" measurement.

◆ Foundation walls should not be more than 1" out of level over the entire surface and not vary more than ½" out of square when measured along a diagonal of 6' × 8' × 10' in any corner.

◆ Leaks resulting in actual trickling of water are unacceptable. Dampness of the walls or floors may occur in new construction and is not considered a deficiency.

◆ It is normal to expect some down-drafting in chimneys during periods of high winds. Some homes may need to have a window opened slightly to create an effective draft for a fireplace because of high energy-conserving construction. (In such cases, an air vent, from the fire box to the outside, is recommended to provide combustion air.)

◆ Chimney separation should not exceed ½″ in any 10″ vertical measurement.

CARPENTRY

◆ Floors shall have no more than ⅜″ ridge or depression within any 32″ measurement running parallel to the joists.

◆ Walls should be curved no more than ¼″ within any 32″ horizontal or vertical measurement and should not be more than ½″ out of plumb in any 8′ vertical measurement.

◆ Changes in humidity will cause natural wood panels to shrink and expand and may expose unpainted surfaces.

◆ Siding should not distort more than ⅛″ in 16″ of run.

◆ Joints in moldings or between moldings and adjacent surfaces should not exceed ⅛″ in width.

◆ Gaps between cabinets and ceilings or walls should not exceed ¼″, and misaligned cabinets should not be greater than 1/16″, providing that the cabinet is structurally secure.

◆ Counter tops must not be more than ¼″ out of level front to rear or in any 8′ of run.

◆ Some warping, especially of exterior doors, is normal but should not exceed ¼″ measured from corner to corner diagonally.

ROOFING

◆ Roofing and flashing should resist leaking under normal conditions.

◆ Shingle edges running parallel to the ridge should vary no more than ½″ from a line parallel to the eave or ridge and stretched from one gable to the adjacent gable.

◆ "Cut Lines" running up the roof should not vary more than ½″ to either side of a line stretched from the eave to the ridge running parallel to the gable.

PLUMBING

◆ Noise emitting from the water pipe system due to the flow of water is acceptable, but noise from loose pipes or water hammer is unacceptable.

◆ Fixture stoppers should hold water a sufficient amount of time to allow for its intended use.

HEATING AND COOLING

◆ The heating system should be capable of producing an inside temperature of 70° when measured in the center of each room at a height of 5′ above the floor under local outdoor winter design conditions.

◆ The cooling system should be capable of maintaining a temperature of 78° when measured in the center of each room at a height of 5′ above the floor under local outdoor summer design conditions. Where outside temperatures exceed 95°, a 15° differential must be maintained.

◆ The temperature in all rooms may vary from 5° to 6°.

◆ When metal ducts are heated and cooled, a normal ticking or crackling sound may exist, but a booming noise caused by "oil canning" is not acceptable.

INSULATION

All areas of walls, floors, and ceilings facing unheated areas should be insulated with a vapor-barrier material that is installed securely. Insulation should be stuffed in openings around ducts, pipes, and wires between heated and unheated areas, and also between framing members and windows and doors.

DRYWALL

Visible nail pops, tape blisters, cracks, and any blemish exceeding ⅛″ is considered unacceptable.

PAINTING

◆ Painted or finished surfaces should present a smooth, unblemished, homogeneous appearance.

◆ Repairs that require repainting should be refinished to match surrounding areas as closely as possible.

GRADING AND DRAINAGE

◆ Ground settlement should not disrupt water drainage away from the structure, although some settlement may occur.

◆ After normal rainfall, water should not stand in the yard or swales or within 10″ of the dwelling for more than 48 hours.

◆ Industry standards have been developed to provide minimum standards for evaluating work that is questionable. *In all cases, a builder's work is expected to meet or exceed these minimum standards.* In many areas covered by these standards, the question of quality is determined by the extent that the work exceeds these standards. Where standard form specifications are established for use with trade contractors, it is not wise to include industry standards, except as a general reference because they represent minimum acceptable conditions of construction, and all builders should seek a higher level of performance.

AMERICAN NATIONAL STANDARDS INSTITUTE

The American National Standards Institute (ANSI) is a private, non-profit membership organization that was founded in 1918 for the purpose of coordinating the U.S. voluntary consensus standards system and approving the American National Standards. ANSI consists of more than 1,300 companies, 30 governmental agencies, and 260 professional, technical, trade, labor, and consumer organizations. In addition to coordinating voluntary standards activities and approving American national standards, ANSI also represents the U.S. interests in international standardization and provides information on, and access to, world standards. American national standards are not mandatory except where they are adopted by governmental agencies by specific reference or where they are specified by contract. Of the almost 10,500 standards approved by ANSI to date, home builders are primarily concerned with the 1,230 that relate to health and safety, and then only when they are referenced as a construction requirement. Copies of specific American National Standards may be purchased through the Institute from catalogues.

INDEX

Page numbers in *italics* denote figures